WISDOM LITERATURE

WISDOM LITERATURE

AN INTRODUCTION

by

JAMES WOOD

Principal and Professor of Systematic Theology
Scottish Congregational College, Edinburgh

GERALD DUCKWORTH & CO. LTD.
3 Henrietta Street, London, W.C.2

Printed in Great Britain
by T. and A. Constable Ltd., Hopetoun Street
Printers to the University of Edinburgh

DEDICATED TO

DAVID N. LOWE, O.B.E., M.A., B.SC., F.R.S.E.

Chairman

and to

WILLIAM N. REDMAN, D.F.C., M.A., F.I.A.

Secretary

and to

WALTER A. BROTCHIE, M.B.E.

Treasurer

of the Scottish Congregational College

CONTENTS

CONTENTS

PREFACE

THIS book aims at interesting both the layman and the student of theology. It has been written to meet some of the needs of those laymen who are ready to ask questions about the meaning of human destiny. That is one reason why, in the opening chapters, numerous extracts from very ancient literature have been quoted. By this method the reader is given some idea of the liveliness and the humour of Wisdom Literature in its early beginnings. By the same method, of course, the student is provided with concrete examples illustrative of the great variety of material within the literature. Many of these extracts are from literature which is not easily available, much of it being quoted directly from scholarly translations of Sumerian, Babylonian, Assyrian and Egyptian Literature.

Readers familiar with older discussions of Wisdom may note with surprise the omission of any detailed discussion of the influence of Greek thought on Hebrew Wisdom Literature. This omission is a common feature of the more recent study on the subject. The Greek influence is probably at its clearest in the Wisdom of Solomon and Ecclesiasticus. But, generally speaking, what previously had been assigned to Greek or Hellenistic influences is now traced back to a very much earlier period. In particular, where Hellenism was supposed to have influenced Wisdom within Judaism, the influence is now related to something much older and more widespread than

Hellenism. It is explained in terms of a cultural outlook characteristic of almost the whole of the ancient Near East; we refer to the Wisdom Movement. Such a movement is an accompaniment of man's civilization. Even in its beginnings it is an expression, on the one hand, of an incipient humanism, with its salty criticism of life, and on the other hand, an awareness of the influence of God, or the gods, on human destiny.

Since a preface is not the place to conduct an argument, I may avoid further discussion of this point by referring to a standard essay on Wisdom Literature written by W. Baumgartner in the composite work *The Old Testament and Modern Study*, edited by H. H. Rowley. He writes (p. 210), 'And now scholars have learnt to see it, too, against the background of the Wisdom of the ancient east. . . . The dependence of Israelite Wisdom on that of Egypt, which had already been recognized by Gunkel, was proved when Erman recognized the original of Prov 22:17–23:11 in the Wisdom book of Amenemope. Our knowledge of Babylonian and Assyrian Wisdom is not so complete, but it was certainly not less significant in either extent or importance. We know how it enriched Greek literature, and that it reached back into Sumerian times.'

One other feature of this volume is the extensive treatment of the New Testament. The tendency in the past has been to bring the subject more or less to a close with the Wisdom of Solomon and Ecclesiasticus, and with some reference to the literary connections between these and the New Testament. I have tried to go a little further, to show how Wisdom thought, no less than its vocabulary, has been utilized in the New Testament expression of its faith in Jesus Christ. In particular, I have suggested that Wisdom has its own kind of contribution to make towards the formulation of a Christology which has any claims to be regarded as adequate.

The author who ventures into the field of Wisdom soon finds he has to work alone. Most recent studies in theology pay some attention to Wisdom literature, but very much less to Wisdom thought, as a necessary element in Biblical theology. Here I have tried, within the limits of a brief work, to make up for this neglect of Wisdom in Biblical studies. The growing interest in theology has not yet paid much attention to the difficulties and subtleties of Wisdom. Several factors seem to operate here. There is, of course, the tendency in much modern theology to emphasize what is frequently called the action of the Living God, particularly as that is seen in the realm of history. But even so welcome a tendency has brought in its train several defects. One of these has been the neglect of the less dramatic, and less historical, contribution from that area of life and experience where Wisdom thought manifests itself. That tendency can be further considered under two heads. First, the emphasis upon the centrality of Revelation has not always avoided the error of a too narrow interpretation of what was meant by revelation. There has been a neglect of some important facets of revelation, such as those wider truths about God which, I believe, are to be seen in the thoughts and reflections of men as they pondered on the mystery of the world and its ways. Now such things are the very staple of Wisdom and have an intrinsic right to be included in any adequate treatment of the Divine revelation. Secondly, the new emphasis upon the Divine transcendence is an advance on that older immanence which seemed at times to blur the lines of distinction between God and man. But this emphasis seems to have rendered suspect the rational element and the immanent view of Deity, so often suggested by Wisdom thought. The cautious note in Wisdom concerning religious experience has suggested to some minds a dangerous anthropocentrism in its thought. But on the other side, the very interest Wisdom has in man's ordinary social and secular life offers, I believe, a corrective to some of the errors to which the new emphasis on transcendence is exposed.

I have had to beware of going to the other extreme and making too great a claim on behalf of Wisdom. But I am strongly of the opinion that a mature Biblical theology must make room for the thoughts and speculations associated with Wisdom. It is hoped that this work may be regarded as a first step towards a re-appraisal of the claims of Wisdom. I have tried to write simply and aimed at interesting the reader in what is, in some respects, a technical and theological subject. However, to lighten the burden of the reader I have relegated to appendices one or two of the more abstract aspects of the subject.

I should like to express thanks to my colleague, Dr W. G. Baker, for the loan of books otherwise difficult to obtain, and to Dr Nathaniel Micklem for his editorial comments, most of which have been incorporated in the text.

Edinburgh, January 1967   J. D. W.

I.—INTRODUCTION

A PROMINENT characteristic of the present age is the great speed at which man pushes outwards the boundaries of knowledge. By means of specialized techniques, and through sheer intellectual power, barriers to scientific progress which were once thought to be immovable have been pushed aside. Examples of the triumphant thrust forward of the human spirit are seen in man's widening knowledge of the world of space beyond the earth's surface, his probing down into the hidden depths of the sea, his study of the microscopic activities within a drop of blood. Satellites are rocketed into the sky and move in a prescribed orbit around the globe; capsules made of newly invented metals fly above the earth, bearing within them instruments which send back information which, in turn, is recorded on a machine operating in a scientist's laboratory. Confidently and inevitably this generation continues to move away from the world our fathers and ancestors lived in. Yet this thrilling story of modern discovery is not quite the whole truth about what is happening in the world today. For at the same time as the human spirit has been eagerly straining forward to obtain greater control of what is popularly called the phenomena of nature, other men, no less modern, no less scientific, and no less representative of the human spirit at its highest, have been stretching out to gain a deeper understanding of how men lived in the world of many centuries ago. At the very time when the modern world has been almost hypnotized by the possibilities which could conceivably open up in the future as the result of scientific progress, there has also been discovered a deeper and truer understanding of what it was to be a human being three, four and five thousand years ago. Such discovery takes us back to the world of bows and arrows, to slavery, magic and astrology, to the world where men moved about on bullock-carts with solid wheels, to that old world where men predicted the future by inspecting the entrails of a ritually sacrificed pigeon, to that world where the art of writing was a new invention. The group of modern men, which has dealt with the ancient past, has not only recovered a knowledge of what men used to do long ago, but has also helped us to see more clearly what went on inside men's heads. These scholars tell us how men behaved in a world where they had to face suffering and death, what questions they asked concerning human destiny and fate, what they thought about God and justice.

Particularly interesting discoveries about the past have been made in recent years in that part of the world usually referred to as the Ancient Near East. It includes Egypt, Palestine and Mesopotamia and the lands adjoining. Through the labours of many scholars, building on the pioneer efforts of their predecessors, there has been rediscovered in our day what is practically a new and unknown world. In a way hardly suspected before, we have been able to learn what men said and thought about life and destiny in the world of at least five thousand years ago. There is now available written evidence to tell us of their hopes and fears, joys and sorrows, pain and well-being, indeed all those experiences which make up human life. The evidence for this claim is based on the newly recovered literature of the Sumerians, the Babylonians and the Egyptians, to mention only the more

obvious names. Quite often, the literature which has
been unearthed has had to be pieced together from
broken fragments, in some cases even the grammar behind the language has had to be worked out. But the
interesting fact is that, on the basis of what has already
been edited and translated, there are now available many
different kinds of compositions in the several literatures.
The variety includes writings as different as stories,
proverbs, fables, lessons for schoolboys, instructions on
etiquette, precepts, hymns, prayers, and wise counsels
from learned instructors. Taken as a whole and with
proper attention to their variety, this literature supplies
a panorama depicting the changing scenes of life. Even
where, as does happen on occasion, the phraseology in
any one particular language (as in Sumerian) seems to be
rather conventional and obviously stereotyped, nevertheless the literature provides an excellent reflection of
life as men knew it in that ancient world.

In a study like this it is impossible to deal with all the
literature available. Our interest is really in that part of
the literature which has connections with what is known
technically as Wisdom Literature. This term is used by
those Old Testament scholars who specialize in literary
criticism. It is used specifically of the three canonical
books, Job, Proverbs and Ecclesiastes. These three are a
sub-group within a larger collection in the Hebrew canon,
known as the Writings. The Hebrew canon as a whole
has three sections known as the Law, the Prophets and
the Writings. By means of a curious system of number-
ing, it is reckoned that there are eleven books in the
Writings. These are Psalms, Song of Songs, Ruth,
Lamentations, Esther, Daniel, Ezra-Nehemiah, Chron-
icles, and the three already named. Acquaintance with
the contents of Job, Proverbs and Ecclesiastes suggests

that it is reasonable to separate these three books from the rather mixed group formed by the other eight, and to give them a special classification, viz. Wisdom Literature. But we cannot strictly limit Wisdom writings to these three books alone; for the characteristics which separate these three from the other eight are the same characteristics which are found elsewhere, scattered here and there in different parts of the Old Testament.

Throughout the Old Testament we come across popular proverbs, wise sayings, aphorisms, observations on animals and plants, fables and precepts. Writings such as these, even although they often look artless and spontaneous, are usually deliberate and well-constructed expressions of what men believed about life. They are really the literary distillations of what they had learned about life through the years. Indeed, they are so true to life that it is difficult to imagine they reflect the experience of only one casual individual speaking, as it were, within the limits of his own short, personal span of life. More probably these writings are the literary precipitate emerging from the gathered wisdom of many generations, during which men have reflected on what it means to be a human being. The sayings we shall be dealing with are the basic raw material out of which Wisdom Literature developed. This original material existed orally in the first instance. It had a public circulation with, presumably, no rights of private ownership. In the course of time, a sifting process took place. Those sayings which possessed the vitality which belongs to the truth about life managed to survive. Later, they were taken over by the learned, preserved and, in some cases, improved upon or given a more polished form, then at a still later stage edited and formed into literary products to become books like Job, Proverbs and Ecclesiastes.

If we are properly to understand Wisdom Literature, we have to see it as the literary side of a living and long-continuing movement. In its most artistic forms, as we have them in the Old Testament and the Apocrypha, the literature embraces human thought at practically all levels. It includes such things as the popular riddles of Samson on the one hand, and the lofty speculations about Wisdom in the book of Job on the other. But taken as a whole, and remembering that the unit of size varies from something as short as 'Is Saul also among the prophets?' (1 Sam 10:12) to a book as long as Proverbs, the Wisdom Literature is in many ways quite distinct from the other writings in the Old Testament. What distinguishes it is the way it thinks about man. It thinks of him as a human being rather than as an Israelite. It deals with him as one person bound in the bundle of life with all men everywhere, and not only with the elect members of God's Chosen Race. It sees him beset with the problems of Everyman rather than as the favoured recipient of priestly instruction. It views him in his setting among other ordinary men rather than as one listening to the inspired voice of the prophet. It looks at him in his business enterprise rather than as performing the prescribed ritual in the Temple. Through its dealing with him in his everyday world rather than in his privileged status as an Israelite, it strikes what might be called a humanist note. But however true it is that the distinctively Israelite note is muted in this literature, this does not obtain throughout the whole period. In the literature outside the canon, and specifically in the Apocrypha, the process of development continued. In the Apocrypha we can discern a development which was probably inherent in Wisdom from its early beginnings. That is, Wisdom becomes increasingly, and indeed explicitly, religious.

In its later literary form, Wisdom proclaims that its inspiration is inseparable from 'the fear of the Lord'. This principle is made fundamental and becomes even more closely integrated into the later teaching of the Bible.

From what has already been said, it will be realized that the range of Wisdom Literature cannot be confined to the Old Testament. As noted above, Wisdom Literature is found in the Apocrypha and is well represented by The Wisdom of Solomon, 'Ecclesiasticus', or, in its alternative title 'The Wisdom of Jesus, the Son of Sirach'. It is found, too, in the New Testament, including some utterances of our Lord, some passages in Paul's Epistles, and, in particular, in the Epistle of James. This, of course, is simply a recognition of the fact that Wisdom belongs to a continuous and widespread movement which was kept alive in Israel (Old and New) for over a thousand years. Also, we have to recognize that the movement is not peculiar to Israel but belongs to the life and culture of the Ancient Near East. We have already alluded to the Wisdom found in Sumeria, Babylon and Egypt, but the Old Testament itself refers to Wisdom found in Teman, Edom, Syria, Shuah and Arabia. Naturally, we shall be most concerned with Wisdom Literature and thought as these are manifested in the Bible, even although it is a fact that there was a Wisdom Movement, with a literature of its own, long before the Bible came into existence. But although Israel borrowed much from surrounding nations and from older cultures, such borrowings represent only the beginning in a long process and not its culmination. For the end-product in Israel, that is, the Wisdom Literature, was distinctive, and in its own rights superior to anything the other nations were ever able to produce. The Wisdom Literature of the Old Testament and the literature derived from it offer to mankind something greater than a technique for cultivating the mind or understanding the phenomena of nature. Seen at its highest and best, this literature is nothing less than one of God's means for preparing man to live in accordance with the Divine will. For reasons such as these, and there are others such as its historical and literary interests, Wisdom Literature is worthy of the attention of the man who is concerned to know about the meaning of life, not only of life in the distant past but in the conditions of today.

II.—WISDOM OUTSIDE ISRAEL:
MESOPOTAMIA (SUMER AND BABYLON)
AND EGYPT

BECAUSE of the wide ramifications of Wisdom Literature
in the Ancient Near East, and because of its continued
existence throughout many centuries before it appeared
in the Old Testament itself, it is necessary to say something, even if briefly, about Wisdom in the lands outside
Israel. This will help us to see in actual fact how widespread was Wisdom, both as a literature and as a way of
viewing life. Also, it will enable us to see the long and
gradual process carried on through the centuries during
which Wisdom, beginning with its secular and very
human presuppositions, comes to be an element used by
God for the enrichment of His self-revelation to mankind. Further, so far as Israel itself is concerned, it will
remind us that although Israel, like the other nations,
adopted the Wisdom techniques as a way of dealing with
life and its problems, yet it took the whole idea of
Wisdom further than any of its predecessors, and used it
at a later stage in its own history to enable man to come
to a deeper understanding of God's way with His world.

The first area we wish to refer to is Mesopotamia, and
in particular to that part which historically has come to
be known as the land of Sumer. The Sumerians were one
of the first of ancient peoples to evolve a system of
writing. They invented the system of inscribing marks or
symbols on clay tablets by means of a stylus. They did

so as early as the third millennium B.C. Not only did the Sumerians invent writing and use it for humble utilitarian purposes, such as keeping Temple accounts, but they used it also to give permanent form to a literature which hitherto had only existed orally. The earliest writings are known to go back to a Classical Sumerian period which may be dated 2500–2400 B.C. This is followed by a different period, where what was Sumerian becomes subjected to Semitic influences. In this newer era a Semitic people, called the Akkadians, took control of Sumer. Their influence is seen in the fact that their Semitic Akkadian inscriptions are written in Sumerian script. The period of time in which this occurred is in the last quarter of the third millennium (2300–2000 B.C.). This, in turn, is succeeded by what might be called a Sumerian Renaissance, which coincides in time with and is a product of what is known as the Third Dynasty of Ur and is dated 2000–1900 B.C. Many new texts were composed in Sumerian at this time. In the centuries which followed, particularly 1700–1600 B.C., there was a marked literary development and many of the Sumerian texts still extant were composed during this period. A little later, 1500–1200 B.C., i.e. the Cassite Period, Babylonian Literature, as distinct from Sumerian, began to flourish. It is in this period that many Sumerian texts were not only copied but also provided with Babylonian translations.

One of the features of this rather chequered history of literature in Mesopotamia is that Sumerian influences are most pervasive. Although it is possible to distinguish Sumerian, Akkadian and Babylonian from each other, yet the dividing line between them is not always easily discernible. Pride of place must be given to Sumerian, especially in its Classical period. For that was the time of very important beginnings, and in particular for the beginning of literature as distinct from the mechanical art of jotting down notes and memoranda. But great credit, too, must be given to the second phase. The Semitic Akkadians were inferior in cultural matters to the Sumerians whom they were ousting as rulers in Mesopotamia. But the defeated Sumerians exerted a strong cultural influence on the Akkadians, so much so that the language in its later form is usually referred to as Sumero-Akkadian. Many of the tablets which have been unearthed and which belong to the Akkadian period naturally show traces of the close literary relations between Sumerians and Akkadians, but at the same time show certain elements which appear to go back to an earlier period. It is a task for the expert philologist to discriminate between the different strands in the language, and does not belong to our purpose here.

In order to avoid the danger of letting this chapter become a technical discussion of the principles of discrimination in the philology of the cuneiform scripts in Mesopotamia or of the different dialects in Egypt, it may be advisable to remind ourselves of what we are aiming at. Quite simply, the aim is to give the reader some idea of what Wisdom Literature is like in these two great centres of culture outside Palestine, namely Mesopotamia and Egypt. Although there are important differences in date and provenance of the Wisdom Literature within each of these two areas, these will not be our main concern, although, of course, these will be noted where necessary. We shall, however, attempt to provide a sufficiently large number of examples of the literature to give the reader some acquaintance with the different kinds of Wisdom Literature written in Mesopotamia and Egypt. We shall add comments here and there, with the intention of explaining obscure points and of drawing attention to interesting features.

We begin with Mesopotamia, and that means the Wisdom Literature of Sumeria. This literature contains interesting examples of proverbs and precepts about human conduct, essays on such subjects as human suffering, fables about animals, and what are called 'Disputations' between rivals, and a number of maxims dealing with life in general; in other words, the kind of writings which we comprehended under the title of Wisdom Literature in our previous chapter.

We begin by drawing attention to a number of proverbs and precepts, some of which go back to a period as early as 1800–1600 B.C. They reflect the ordinary outlook of observant people who are aware of the things that make for success in life. The Sumerians were sufficiently literary-minded to gather proverbs into collections, which implies, of course, a certain degree of editorial activity. There is a high degree of probability that some of the proverbs we are about to quote were in circulation orally early in the second millennium B.C.

'As long as a man does not exert himself, he will gain nothing.'

'Friendship lasts a day,
Kinship endures forever.'

'A joyful heart: the bride.
A sorrowful heart: the groom.'

'The state weak in armaments—
The enemy will not be driven from its gates.'

The other side of the picture is seen in another proverb:

'You go and carry off the enemy's land;
The enemy comes and carries off your land.'

'You can have a lord, you can have a king,
But the man to fear is the tax collector.'

But Sumerian Wisdom contains more than popular proverbs; it also provides examples of sustained treatment of profound subjects. One of outstanding importance is an essay on the problem of human suffering. In its original form it may be as early as 2000 B.C. In its extant form as reconstructed by modern scholars it is usually dated 1700 B.C. It is written in poetry and has been pieced together from fragments. It bears a resemblance to the Book of Job. There is an edition of it by S. N. Kramer, in the Supplement to the *Vetus Testamentum*, volume III, 1955. Kramer has given it the title 'A Sumerian Variation on the "Job" motif'. Not all editors of this text are in agreement as to the subject. It is at least a dialogue between a man and his god, but there is room for doubt as to whether the man was righteous in the sense that Job was righteous. But there is no doubt about the interest of its contents. The text begins by exhorting men to praise their God:

'Let a human being utter constantly the exaltedness of his god,
Let a man praise artlessly the words of his god.'

The second part of the poem begins at line 10 and introduces the speaker but does not name him:

'The (?) man—he uses not his strength for evil in (?) the place of deceit.'

The third part begins at what would be line 21, but some lines are missing and it only becomes clear at line 26:

'I am a man, a discerning one, (yet) who respects (?) me prospers (?) not,
My righteous word has been turned into a lie.'

This third section continues as far as line 116 and contains what may be (but it is not certain) a confession of sin at line 111:

'My god, now that you have shown (?) me my sins. . . .'

and at line 113,

'I, the man, would confess (?) my sins before you.'

From this point to the end of this section the worshipper pleads for help from his god.

The last section, lines 117–131, forms a happy ending. The divine answer is apparently favourable, and, if the translation can be trusted, the worshipper's sorrow is turned into joy—lines 126, 127 and 130:

'The (demon of) fate, who had been placed (there) in accordance (?) with his sentence (?), he turned aside (?), He turned the (m)an's (?) suffering into joy, (The man uttered) constantly the exaltedness of his god.'

Such a poem suggests a comparison with the Book of Job. Just how closely they are related is difficult to say. However, this poem precedes Job by more than a thousand years. It shows that Sumerian thinkers were concerned with the problems of suffering and adversity. In this poem we see how the writer had to work within the theological framework of his day. The god he calls upon is probably a minor deity, sometimes described as a 'personal god'—in distinction from the major gods who were too exalted to be directly concerned with the affairs of human beings. The 'personal god' acted as a go-between and represented the human being in the assembly of the Sumerian gods. According to that kind of thinking about the gods, the sensible procedure for a man in adversity was to submit as quickly as possible to the will of the gods. Man was helpless before the gods' inscrutable will. The sufferer here has no thought of arguing his innocence, like Job, before the gods. Man had no righteousness of his own to plead in his defence; indeed, the contrary was the case. The poem teaches explicitly, lines 102–103:

'Never has a sinless child been born to its mother,
. . . a sinless workman (?) has not existed from of old.'

On this view, misfortune and suffering are caused by man's sinfulness, which, in turn, is an inescapable element in human nature. But the very fact of a wisdom poem like this is fairly good evidence that not all Sumerian thinkers were satisfied with the conventional theology. Despite the readiness of the sufferer to acquiesce in the mysterious will of the gods, there is an implicit protest against his having to suffer at the hand of the gods. It may well be that the poem had for one of its purposes the aim of warning man against the habit of criticizing the gods for the way they dealt with human beings. This would help to account for that rather flat and conventional ending of the poem where one might have hoped for some bolder conclusion.

In addition to dealing with problems in the relations between man and God there are examples of fables based on animal lore. These fables deal with many different animals. The most frequently mentioned are the dog, cat, cattle, donkey, fox, pig, sheep, ox, goat and wolf. One or two examples will illustrate how the Sumerians handled this kind of Wisdom writing:

'A cat—for its thoughts;
A mongoose—for its actions.'

'The donkey eats its own bedding.'

'The fox gnashes its teeth, but its head is trembling.'

Some of these proverbs grew in size and show an early stage in the process which led to the creation of the miniature essay, e.g.

'The pork-butcher slaughters the pig, saying:

"Must you squeal? This is the road which your sire and your grandsire travelled, and now you are going on it too, (and yet) you are squealing!"'

Another type of Wisdom composition is a special kind of essay, called the Disputation. The idea behind it is of a contest between rivals. The rivals may be persons, or things, such as minerals like copper and silver, or seasons, such as summer and winter, or different professions like farmer and shepherd. Some see in the Disputation a style of writing which has affinities with the Cain and Abel story in the Book of Genesis. For our purposes, its interest lies in the fact that it seems to preserve reflections on differences between things. The Disputation is an early attempt to evaluate men, materials, phenomena of nature. It is a technique for obtaining a fuller understanding of the conditions under which men lived. A charming example of this type is told in the form of an agricultural myth. It concerns a goddess Inanna, her brother Utu, a shepherd-god named Dumuzi and a farmer-god named Enkimdu. Utu urges his sister to marry the shepherd but she refuses and marries the farmer. This leads to a disputation between the farmer and the shepherd. It is possible that behind the myth is a 'disputation' concerning the relative values of the two different occupations in Sumerian society. In this example the two rivals are reconciled. This may imply that Sumerian society accepted both the shepherd and the farmer as being necessary and that both had their rightful places in the larger whole of civilized life.

Near the end of the poem we see how Enkimdu, representing the farmer, refuses to quarrel with Dumuzi, representing the shepherd:

'I against you, shepherd, against you shepherd, I against you, Why shall I strive?'

The shepherd is appeased and replies:

'Farmer Enkimdu, as my friend, farmer, as my friend, May you be counted as my friend.'

Obviously the brief extracts quoted above cannot give the full flavour of Sumerian Wisdom. But possibly they will indicate the many different kinds of Wisdom Literature which circulated in Sumer. An equally great variety of form and of subject-matter characterizes Babylonian Wisdom Literature. This is, of course, only to be expected as there is a most intimate connection between the two literatures and it is possible to regard the Babylonian as being a continuation of the Sumerian. The variety shows itself quite clearly in the way the editor of the standard work, *Babylonian Wisdom Literature*, W. G. Lambert, has grouped his material under eight heads, such as (1) a Poem, (2) a Theodicy, (3) Precepts and Admonitions, (4) Hymns, (5) Dialogue, (6) Fables and Contest Literature, (7) Popular Sayings and (8) Proverbs. It is possible that on a more precise definition of what is meant by Wisdom Literature, some of these items may be classified as Wisdom only with some degree of hesitation. But for our purposes all that is required is that we select a sufficient number of items to illustrate the nature of the literature. We propose therefore to begin with what are classified as Popular Sayings. These sayings contain fables about animals and insects. They are brief, usually amusing and probably didactic or moral in aim.

'The pig is not fit for a temple, lacks sense, is not allowed to tread on pavements,
An abomination to all the gods, an abhorrence (to (his) God,) accursed by Shamash.'

This may be regarded as an expression of the Semitic dislike of the pig.

'A mouse, out of the way of a mongoose, entered a snake's hole.
He said, "A snake-charmer sent me. Greetings!"'

This may be regarded as an example of presence of mind.

'The fowler who had no fish, but (had caught) birds,
Holding his bird net jumped into the city moat.'

This is a satirical observation on those who manifest an inability to adjust themselves to new situations.

'The sycophant stands in court at the city gate,
Right and left he hands out bribes.
The warrior Shamash knows his misdeeds.'

A reminder that the god Shamash opposes bribery.

The following examples of '*Proverbs*' show a certain practical wisdom in the affairs of daily life:

'When you exert yourself, your god is yours. When you do not exert yourself, your god is not yours.'

To 'have a god' means to be successful. This proverb seems to be an exhortation to self-effort.

'The wise man is girded with a loin-cloth. The fool is clad in a scarlet cloak.'

'When you have seen the profit of reverencing (your) god, you will praise (your) god and salute the king.'

The Babylonians expected material benefits from religion. It is interesting to see the close connection between the god and the king.

There is a collection of moral exhortations known as the 'Counsels of Wisdom'. It is 166 lines in length although some of these are incomplete. It is made up of 10 sections, each dealing with a specific topic. They are (1) the evils of bad company, (2) indiscreet speech, (3) avoidance of litigation, (4) justice to enemies, (5) courtesy and kindness, (6) female company, (7) behaviour towards a prince, (8) careless talk, (9) religious duties, (10) trustworthiness.

The counsels are addressed to 'my son', a common expression in Wisdom Literature which may be either a son or a pupil. The collection may have been composed in the Cassite Period (1500–1200 B.C.) and probably incorporates oral traditions as well as popular literary material. The warnings against female company show resemblances to the Book of Proverbs.

The following examples illustrate the contents of the Counsels:

'Let your mouth be controlled and your speech guarded:
Therein is a man's wealth—let your lips be very precious.'

'Do not frequent a law court,
Do not loiter where there is a dispute.'

'Do not honour a slave girl in your house;
She shall not rule (your) bedroom like a wife.'

'My son, if it be the wish of the prince that you are his,
If you attach his closely guarded seal to your person
Open his treasure house, enter within

But do not covet any of this,
Nor set your mind on double-dealing.'
'Do not utter solemn oaths while alone.'

This may indicate that walls have ears.

'Do not speak hypocrisy, (utter) what is decent.'

As distinct from short sayings of no more than a line
or two, and from brief stanzas as in the Counsels of
Wisdom, there are also more extended compositions.
There is a notable monologue entitled 'The Poem of the
Righteous Sufferer'. In an earlier generation this was
sometimes described as the 'Babylonian Job', but this is
a misnomer and a better title would be the one suggested
by Lambert (*op. cit.*, p. 27) 'The Babylonian Pilgrim's
Progress'. In its original form it may have been from
400 to 500 lines in length. The speaker is Subsi-Mesre-
Sakkan and he addresses the 'Lord of Wisdom', i.e. the
Babylonian god Marduk. The speaker has been a man of
authority and of exemplary piety. But he has been forsaken by the king, rejected by the gods, disowned by
friends and despised by slaves. All kinds of diseases
afflict him and he gives way to despair. His sufferings
seem to have been imposed on him by Marduk. Later,
three dreams are vouchsafed him. In the first he sees a
young man, in the second a priest, and in the third a
young woman who looks like a queen or a goddess.
These visitants indicate that Marduk will restore the
sufferer to health and wealth. The cure takes place in
stages and ends in complete restoration. The following
quotations will illustrate the style of writing. The opening line is, 'I will praise the lord of Wisdom . . .'.

'My god has forsaken me and disappeared,
My goddess has failed me and keeps at a distance.

'I, who strode along as a noble, have learned to slip by
unnoticed.
Though a dignitary, I have become a slave.'

'The day of the goddess's procession was profit and
gain to me.'

The Babylonians expected religion to be profitable.

'The exorcist has not diagnosed the nature of my
complaint,
Nor has the diviner put a time limit on my illness.'

'The Babylonians saw how (Marduk) restores to life,
and all quarters extolled his greatness.'

'Who but Marduk restores his dead to life?
Apart from Sarpanitum, which goddess grants life?'

'The protecting genius and the guardian spirit, divine
attendants of the brickwork of Esagil
(——) —libation I made their hearts glow,
(With) the succulent (meals) I made them exultant.'

The 'brickwork of Esagil' refers to the temple of Marduk.

Another interesting example, where a subject is treated
extensively, is one called 'The Babylonian Theodicy'. It
has been likened both to the Book of Job and the Book
of Ecclesiastes, but the resemblances are not close. It is
a poem of 27 stanzas, each stanza having 11 lines. In
each stanza, every line begins with the same sign. The
resultant 27 signs, when put together, form an acrostic,
which, when the lost letters have been restored, give the
name and profession of the author.

'I, Saggil-kinam-ukkib, the incantation priest, am
adorant of the god and king' (Lambert, 63).

It was written about 1000 B.C., and there is a commentary
on it, which suggests that it dealt with a subject of
interest to educated people in Babylon.

The theme of the poem is introduced in the third stanza where the sufferer says to his friend,

'I will ask you a question; listen to me,
  Pay attention for a moment; hear my words.'

The phrases used here are quite stereotyped and are often used with an introductory aim. The real beginning is in the two immediately following lines,

'My body is a wreck, emaciation darkens (me),
  My success has vanished, my stability has gone.'

The friend hardly knows how to reply but ventures the suggestion that the fault is not in the sufferer; that it is bound up with the fact that the plans of the gods are hidden from mortals.

'You are as stable as the earth, but the plan of the gods
  is remote.'

He adds to this pious utterance some observations about retribution falling upon the wicked:

'Come, consider the lion that you mentioned, the
  enemy of the cattle. For the crime which the lion
  committed the pit awaits him.'

It is possible that 'lion' and 'cattle' are metaphorical. The friend frequently appeals to conventional ideas and later on in the poem says, in the same strain,

'The godless cheat who has wealth,
  A death-dealing weapon pursues him.'

Naturally, the sufferer is not convinced and points to the injustices he has observed:

'I have looked around society, but the evidence is
  contrary.
  The god does not impede the way of a devil.'

B

and asserts he has received no advantage from being religious.

> 'How have I profited that I have bowed down to my god?
> I have to bow beneath the base fellow that meets me;
> The dregs of humanity, like the rich and opulent, treat me with contempt.'

The conclusion reached is that blame for injustice in human life is due to the gods. They have made human beings in such a way that they behave unjustly.

> 'Narru, king of the gods, who created mankind,
> And majestic Zulammar, who dug out their clay
> And mistress Mami, the queen who fashioned them,
> Gave perverse speech to the human race.
> With lies, and not truth, they endowed them for ever.'

Mami is another name for Enlil, one of the chief gods. Zulammar is another name for Ea, who also is one of the chief gods. Mami is the Mother goddess. These lines preserve a criticism of the gods. The poem begins with the assumption that the functions of the gods were to preserve justice, prosper the righteous and bring retribution upon the wicked. But such functions are hardly consistent with the teaching here that men do evil because gods have made them behave in that way.

There is a unique composition known as the 'Dialogue of Pessimism'. It is difficult to estimate its date, but it is a late composition rather than early. Some 84 lines have been preserved. It is best understood as a satire on pessimism and it is probably meant to be taken seriously. It purports to be a discussion between a master and his slave. The subject is the futility of life, and, in a manner of great interest to the psychologist, it depicts how the frustrated mind never brings any project to a conclusion.

Whatever line of action the master proposes, he no sooner announces it than he finds an excuse for not doing it. He is aided and abetted by his slave in this process of never prosecuting an action. When the master says he will do something, the slave immediately approves the action; then, when the master changes his mind, the slave at once encourages him not to do the action. The master passes in quick review the advantages of certain courses of action but rejects each one in turn as soon as he has mentioned it. He speaks of riding in his chariot, dining, hunting, rearing a family, leading a revolution, loving a woman, offering a sacrifice, lending money and food, benefiting his country, committing suicide. As a result of this repeated denial of the value of action, there comes inevitably the denial of all values and the rejection of all good. Two quotations will illustrate the nature of the poem:

> 'Slave (listen) to me.'
> 'Here I am, sir, here I am.'
> 'Quickly (fetch) me water for my hands, and give it to me so that I can dine.'
> 'Dine, sir, dine. Repeated dining relaxes the mind.'
> '— (——) —his god's repast: Shamash accompanies washed hands.'
> 'No, (slave), I will certainly not dine.
> Hunger and eating, thirst and drinking, come upon a man.'

The same formula runs through most of the stanzas in the poem. The last stanza, with its reference to suicide, carries with it the suggestion that the slave is probably mocking the master.

> 'Slave, listen to me.'
> 'Here I am, sir, here I am.'

'What, then, is good?'
'To have my neck and your neck broken,
 And to be thrown into the river is good.'
'Who is so tall as to ascend to the heavens?
 Who is so broad as to compass the underworld?'
'No, slave, I will kill you and send you first.'
'And my master would certainly not outlive me by
 even three days.'

The quotation used by the slave in his reply,

'Who is so tall as to ascend to the heavens?
 Who is so broad as to compass the underworld?'

naturally expects a negative answer, and this fits in with
the pessimism which is ready to accept the idea of
suicide. The quotation itself seems to be a proverb. It
expresses the view that man lacks the greatness which is
necessary to make him capable of dealing with the
problems he meets in life.

It is hoped that the above extracts from the Wisdom
Literature of Mesopotamia will have given some idea of
the nature of the literature. There are differences of
various kinds. For example, differences of form are
obvious in that in size alone, it varies from the single line
up to the lengthy poem. Also, there are stanzas of 2, 3
and 4 lines in length. Then there are connected stanzas
which together form a relatively lengthy poem. Parallel
with these differences in length of compositions there are
differences, too, in subject-matter. There are the simple,
one-line-long, wise utterances. There are proverbs of
varying lengths. There are what can be called 'miniature
essays'. Also, there are lengthy, sustained treatments of
subjects of ethical and philosophical interest. The
Wisdom Literature seems to change its size and change
its subject-matter because it is so closely and intimately

bound up with man's changing needs in life itself. Where, for example, a witty wisecrack is all that is required, it is, sooner or later, given literary form. Where a slightly more elaborate utterance is required, the wise man will give it literary expression. Where instruction is required, especially for the inculcation of a professional skill, then the demand is supplied by the wise teacher. Where mature men reflect on life, with all its changes and chances, its weal and woe, then the reflective poem emerges.

In its different forms Wisdom Literature is brought into the closest possible contact with life itself. It is true, of course, that the literature undergoes polishing and development, and the earliest writings are frequently shaped and adapted to suit new and later situations; but that, naturally enough, only underlines the closeness of the relation between the literature and the life from which it springs.

Egyptian Wisdom Literature

Wisdom Literature makes an early appearance in the history of Egypt. In its earliest form it appears largely as wise sayings. These sayings aimed at providing instruction on how to make a success of life. Indeed, instruction or teaching which aimed at success in life is just what wisdom means in this earlier stage. An outstanding example of this kind of wisdom is 'The Instruction of the Vizier Ptah-hotep' which was written in the third millennium B.C. Its contents are mainly practical and popular. At a later period, another kind of Wisdom writing emerged. The difference between the two is that the later form prefers a longer and more connected treatment of a subject rather than a compilation of

relatively short sayings. A good example of this kind is
'The Dispute over Suicide'. Here, of course, we have a
different attitude to life. The literature is set against a
less optimistic background; there is an increased doubt
concerning conventional values in life. This kind of
composition was produced about the beginning of the
second millennium B.C. It is characterized by the importance it attaches to ethical and religious standards. It
counsels submission to the wise, gracious providence of
the god Re. The human ideal is the tranquil sage who
manifests wisdom in all his ways.

We propose to make reference to seven examples of
Egyptian Wisdom writings in order to show something
of the great variety there is within it. Naturally, quotations from these writings[1] will be the briefest possible.
Yet, even on the basis of this slight selection it will be
seen that Egyptian Wisdom shares certain things in
common with Mesopotamian. Principally, what is
common is the rather keen and critical look at life itself.
There is an attempt to come to terms with what today
we should call the human situation. The writings from
these two great areas of human culture deal with how
men actually behave, with what they actually believe
about God, and what they actually think is valuable in
life. This generalization is seen to apply to Mesopotamian and Egyptian Wisdom and no less to Hebrew
Wisdom. However, this is only to be expected if, as we
shall see later, Wisdom Literature is international rather
than national, and if in the Ancient Near East there was
a widespread movement in educated circles to collect
and put into literary form, the lessons men were learning
from life, whatever their nationality.

---

[1] *Ancient Near Eastern Texts* (2nd Ed.), Pritchard.

The Instruction of the Vizier Ptah-Hotep

This is a compilation attributed to Ptah-hotep, the vizier of King Izezi (2450 B.C.). The title 'Instruction' (or 'Teaching') is the Egyptian equivalent of 'Wisdom' and it takes the form of instructions for a royal official. It purports to have been written for the benefit of the son of Ptah-hotep who became his successor in office. It deals with all the problems likely to beset a high officer in the royal service. But it will be noticed that domestic and personal matters also come within the scope of wisdom. This first extract is addressed to the king.

'Let a command be issued to this servant' (i.e. Ptah-hotep himself) 'to make a staff of old age,' (i.e. his son as his support) 'that my son may be made to stand in my place. Then may I speak to him the words of them that listen and the ideas of the ancestors, of them that hearken to the gods. Then shall the like be done for thee, that strife may be banished from the people and the Two Banks[1] may serve thee.'

The king replies in the following manner:

'Teach thou him first about speaking. Then he may set an example for the children of officials. May obedience enter into him, and all heart's poise. Speak to him. There is no one born wise.'

The practical nature of the teaching can be seen from the following:

'Let not thy heart be puffed-up because of thy knowledge; be not confident because thou art a wise man. Take counsel with the ignorant as well as the wise.'

---

[1] i.e. The banks of the River Nile.

'If thou art a man of intimacy, whom one great man sends to another, be thoroughly reliable when he sends thee. Carry out the errand for him as he has spoken. Do not be reserved about what is said to thee, and beware of (any) act of forgetfulness. Grasp hold of truth and do not exceed it.'

'If thou desirest to make friendship last in a home to which thou hast access as master, as a brother, or as a friend, into any place where thou mightest enter, beware of approaching the women.'

'Bow thy back to thy superior, thy overseer from the palace.'

'How good it is when a son accepts what his father says! Thereby maturity comes to him. He whom God loves is a hearkener, (but) he whom God hates cannot hear.'

'As for the fool who does not hearken, he cannot do anything. He regards knowledge as ignorance and profit as loss. He does everything blameworthy, so that one finds fault with him every day. He lives on that through which he should die, and guilt is his food. His character therefrom is told as something known to the officials.'

A Dispute over Suicide

This work was composed *c.* 2280–2000 B.C., and probably expressed the despondent mood of men who were critical of conventional moral and religious beliefs. It is some 155 lines in length, but the beginning is lost. It takes the form of a dialogue between a man and his soul. The man is weary of life and contemplates suicide. His soul disagrees with this idea. A feeling of disillusionment pervades the poem, which is in contrast with the generally optimistic outlook of Egyptians, among whom even death was regarded as a condition that could lead to enjoyment in the world beyond.

Near the beginning of the extant text the man expresses impatience with his own attempts to convince his soul of the desirability of suicide:

> 'My soul is stupid to (try to) win over one wretched over life and delay me from death before I come to it. Make the West' (i.e. land of the dead) 'pleasant for me! Is that (so) bad? Life is a circumscribed period: (even) the trees must fall.'

There then follow four short poems where the man and his soul continue the argument. The man says, 'my name will reek' if he accepts the advice of his soul; he has no congenial friends:

> 'One's fellows are evil;
> The friends of today do not love.'

Death seems attractive to him:

> 'Death is in my sight today
> Like the odour of myrrh,
> Like sitting under an awning on a breezy day.'

and lastly, the dead share the privileges of the gods:

> 'Why surely he who is yonder
> Will be a living god,
> Punishing a sin of him who commits it.'

The argument ends with the soul agreeing with the man about suicide and expressing its readiness to share in his fate:

> 'Whether it be desirable that I (remain) here (because) thou hast rejected the West, or whether it is desirable that thou reach the West and thy body join the earth, I shall come to rest after thou hast relaxed (in death). Thus shall we make a home together.'

The Instruction of King Meri-Ka-Re

This was composed by King Wah-ka-re Khety II, the father of Meri-ka-re, who succeeded him on the throne. Its date is 2100 B.C. It contains shrewd political comments, but the main interests are justice and personal conduct.

> 'Be a craftsman in speech, (so that) thou mayest be strong, (for) the tongue is a sword to (a man), and speech is more valorous than any fighting.'

> 'Copy thy fathers and thy ancestors. . . . Behold, their words remain in writing. Open, that thou mayest read and copy (their) wisdom. (Thus) the skilled man becomes learned.'

> 'Do justice whilst thou endurest upon earth. Quiet the weeper; do not oppress the widow; supplant no man in the property of his father; and impair no officials at their posts. Be on thy guard against punishing wrongfully. Do not slaughter; it is not of advantage to thee.'

The next extract refers to judgment after death by a tribunal of gods, probably with the sun-god as president. These judges know all the sins committed by men and not even the passing of time will cause them to forget:

> 'The council which judges the deficient, thou knowest that they are not lenient on that day of judging the miserable, the hour of doing (their) duty. It is woe when the accuser is one of knowledge. Do not trust in length of years, for they regard a lifetime as (but) an hour. A man remains over after death, and his deeds are placed beside him in heaps. However, existence yonder is for eternity, and he who complains of it is a fool. (But) as for him who reaches it without wrong-

doing, he shall exist yonder like a god, stepping out freely like the lords of eternity.'

Our final quotation draws attention to some aspects of what might be called Egyptian Wisdom Theology. It gives a special title to the god, i.e. 'the Lord of the Hand'. This probably suggests his creative power. He is regarded as invisible, and as in control of all things. Men are told of the importance of a properly equipped tomb, and of the kind of moral and ritual behaviour which leads to life beyond death.

'Generation passes generation among men, and the god who knows (men's) characters has hidden himself. (But) there is none who can withstand the Lord of the Hand; he is one who attacks what the eyes can see . . . also the soul goes to the place which it knows, and deviates not from its way of yesterday. Enrich thy house of the West; embellish thy place of the necropolis, as an upright man and as one who executes the justice upon which (men's) hearts rely. More acceptable is the character of one upright of heart than the ox of the evildoer. Act for the god, that he may act similarly for thee, with oblations, which make the offering table flourish and with a carved inscription—that is what bears witness to thy name. The god is aware of him who acts for him.'

Instruction of Amen-Em-Opet

This is closely related to parts of the Book of Proverbs, especially chapters 22:17–24:22. It is 155 lines in length and is divided into 30 chapters. The original may have been composed about 1300 B.C., and was in popular demand for many centuries. The teaching is on a higher moral and religious level than most of the earlier Egyptian

Wisdom. It sets forth the ideal of the sage, that is the wise, tranquil man who guards his tongue and seeks to meet the demands of morality and religion in his daily conduct.

Old Testament scholars have noted the resemblances between this composition and the Book of Proverbs. The degree of resemblance varies from part to part. In some cases, it is probable that both Amen-Em-Opet and the Book of Proverbs drew upon a common stock of Wisdom sayings which were current in the Ancient Near East. In other cases, especially at Proverbs 22:17–24:22, the more probable explanation of the resemblances between the two is that Proverbs is dependent on the Egyptian work. For here the resemblance is not only in contents but also in the order in which the items are written. Also, some obscure passages in the Hebrew text can be clarified by recourse to the Egyptian. The outstanding example is Proverbs 22:20. Here, the first line (in the R.V.) reads: 'Have I not written unto thee excellent things . . .?', with a marginal note saying that 'excellent things' might be translated as 'heretofore'. The text of Amen-em-Opet supplies the true reading, as rendered now by the R.S.V.: 'Have I not written for you thirty sayings . . .?' This amended reading 'thirty sayings' fits in also with the fact that Amen-em-Opet itself is composed of 30 sections. It is further claimed that Proverbs 22:17–24:22 itself (apart from the introductory verses, 22:17–21) is composed of 30 sections.

The text is a lengthy one of 531 lines, and is divided into 30 chapters. The present text is usually dated about 1000 B.C., but the original may have been as early as 1300 B.C. Parts of the composition were used as exercises in writing for schoolboys in Egyptian schools. The author describes himself as a scribe, or possibly as the son of a scribe and he addresses his compilation to his son. The preface to the work gives a good idea of its aim:

'The beginning of the teaching of life, the testimony for prosperity, all precepts for intercourse with elders, the rules for courtiers, to know how to return an answer to him who said it, and to direct a report to one who has sent him, in order to direct him to the ways of life, to make him prosper upon earth, let his heart go down into its shrine, steer him away from evil, and to rescue him from the mouth of the rabble, revered in the mouth of the people;
Made by the Overseer of the Soil, one experienced in his office, the seed of a scribe of Egypt . . .'

Thereafter many different topics are discussed, such as prudence in argument, honesty and tranquillity, search for wealth, dignity, false weights, reticence, respect for infirmity, benevolence, etc.

The following five extracts will illustrate the contents and style of writing:

'Do not carry off the landmark at the boundaries of the arable land,
Nor disturb the position of the measuring-cord;
Be not greedy after a cubit of land,
Nor encroach upon the boundaries of a widow. . . .'

'Do not associate to thyself the heated man,
Nor visit him for conversation.
Preserve thy tongue from answering thy superior,
And guard thyself from reviling him.'

'Do not lean on the scales nor falsify the weights,
Nor damage the fractions of the measure.
Do not wish for a (common) country measure
And neglect those of the treasury.
The ape sits beside the balance
And his heart is in the plummet.

Which God is as great as Thoth,
He that discovered these things, to make them?
Make not for thyself weights which are deficient:
They abound in grief through the will of the god.'

It should be pointed out that the ape was sacred to Thoth who was a god of wisdom and a judge.

'One thing are the words which men say,
Another is that which the god does.'

This is equivalent to 'man proposes, God disposes'.

The final section sums up the advantages to be derived from the wisdom taught by Amen-em-Opet;

'See thou these thirty chapters:
They entertain; they instruct;
They are foremost of all books;
They make the ignorant to know.
If they are read out before the ignorant,
Then he will be cleansed by them.
Fill thyself with them; put them in thy heart,
And be a man who can interpret them,
Who will interpret them as a teacher.
As for the scribe who is experienced in his office,
He will find himself worthy (to be) a courtier.'

In Praise of Learned Scribes

The text is dated 1300 B.C. and describes the advantages of being a professional scribe. It claims that through writing a man achieves immortality. This work was used as a textbook to train boys in writing and doubtless it kept before them the importance of diligence in their studies. The opening paragraph is as follows:

'Now then, if thou dost these things, thou art skilled in the writings. As for those learned scribes from the time of those who lived after the gods, they who could foretell what was to come, their names have become everlasting, (even although) they are gone, they completed their lives, and all their relatives are forgotten.'

'More effective is a book than the house of the builder or tombs in the West. It is better than a (well-)founded castle or a stela in a temple.'

The Satire on the Trades

This should be seen as a contrast with the preceding one on the advantages of being a scribe. It may come from a time somewhere between 2150 and 1750 B.C. It praises the scribal profession and downgrades trades. The author is said to be Khety, son of Duauf, and he wrote for the benefit of his son Pepy.

'I have seen how the belaboured man is belaboured— thou shouldst set thy heart in pursuit of writing. And I have observed how one may be rescued from his duties—behold, there is nothing which surpasses writing. . . .'

The following extracts refer to some of the trades which the scribe regarded with disdain:

'The Barber is (still) shaving at the end of dusk. When he gives himself up to chins, he puts himself upon his (own) shoulder. He gives himself from street to street, to seek out whom he may shave. Thus if he is valiant his arms will fill his belly, like a bee eating for its work.'

'The embalmer, his fingers are foul, for the odour thereof is (that of) corpses. His eyes burn from the greatness of the heat. He could not oppose his own daughter. He spends the day cutting up old rags, so that clothing is an abomination to him.'

'Behold, there is no profession free of a boss—except for the scribe: he is the boss.'

'Behold, I have set thee on the way of God. The Renenut of a scribe is on his shoulder on the day of his birth. He reaches the halls of the magistrates, when he has become a man. Behold, there is no scribe who lacks food, from the property of the House of the King—life, prosperity, health! Meskhenet is (the source of) the scribe's welfare, he being set before the magistrates. His father and mother praise God, he being set upon the way of the living.'

It should be noted that 'Renenut' was a goddess of fortune and that she had favoured the scribe from his birth. Meskhenet also was a goddess and presided over birth and destiny.

The Instruction of Ani

Here, again, a father passes on 'Wisdom' to his son. Ani instructs his son to follow the ideal of the quiet, self-controlled man. This is an ideal which came into prominence nearer the end of the Egyptian Empire and a probable date for the text is about 1000 B.C. Elements of a religious and cultic nature are emphasized, as the first quotation will show:

'Celebrate the feast of thy god and repeat it at its season. God is angry at them who disregard him. Have witnesses attending when thou makest offering at the first time of doing it. . . .'

'Be on thy guard against a woman from abroad, who is not known in her (own) town. Do not stare at her when she passes by. . . .'

'Thou shouldst not express thy (whole) heart to the stranger, to let him discover thy speech against thee. If a passing remark issuing from thy mouth is hasty and it is repeated, thou wilt make enemies. A man may fall to ruin because of his tongue. . . .'

Additional Samples of Wisdom Literature

So far we have drawn our examples from the two chief areas where Wisdom Literature is found, Mesopotamia and Egypt. But, as has been pointed out, Wisdom Literature belongs to a widespread movement rather than to any one localized area. Although we have spoken of Sumerian, Babylonian, Egyptian and Hebrew Wisdom, these are not to be thought of as separate and parallel literatures which have no connection with one another. On the contrary, the very nature of Wisdom Literature is that it tends to overleap national boundaries. Since it was a literature which dealt with man as man, rather than as a Sumerian or Babylonian or Egyptian or Hebrew, there was a tendency for Wisdom writers to use examples of it, wherever they found it, for their own purposes. A good illustration of this tendency is the composition known as *The Words of Ahiqar*. Versions of this work are found in different languages, in different parts of the world and in many different centuries. It may have originated in the seventh century B.C. in the Assyrian Empire of Sennacherib, but it is found also in Christian times in Syriac, Arabic, Armenian and Slavonic versions. A well-known version (or part of it) is in Aramaic, which was written in the fifth century B.C. and was found among the Elephantiné Papyri. It has points of contact with the Old Testament, in the Psalms, Proverbs and Ecclesiastes, and with the Apocrypha in the book of Tobit.

Ahiqar was a high official under Sennacherib. He had no son but adopted Nadan his nephew and trained him to become his successor. The Wisdom sayings, which are only part of the larger work, purport to be the wisdom-lore which Ahiqar imparted to his nephew.[1] The sayings show resemblances to the Psalms, Proverbs and Ecclesiastes, as well as Ecclesiasticus. Recent studies are less inclined to assert dependence of the Biblical material on Ahiqar, and prefer to explain resemblances on the view that both had access to a common stock of wisdom. It is probable that Ahiqar itself can be traced back to a Mesopotamian source. It is probable, too, that in relation to the Book of Proverbs, some sections can be traced to Canaanite predecessors rather than to Ahiqar. The resemblances are not due to borrowing, one from the other, but to both having access to common materials mediated through different channels. The following extracts will illustrate the kind of wisdom found in Ahiqar:

'Hear, O my son Nadan, and come to the understanding of me, and be mindful of my words, as the words of God.'

'My son, it is better to remove stones with a wise man than to drink wine with a fool.'

'My son, envy not the prosperity of thy enemy; and rejoice not at his adversity.'

'My son, the words of a liar are like fat sparrows; and he that is void of understanding eateth them.'

'My son, sweeten thy tongue and make savoury the opening of thy mouth.'

'My son, if the waters should stand up without earth, and the sparrow fly without wings, and the raven become white as snow and the bitter become sweet as honey, then may the fool become wise.'

'My son, thou hast been to me like the dog that came to the potter's oven to warm himself, and after he was warm rose up to bark at them.'

[1] Quoted from the Syriac version as in *Apocrypha and Pseudepigrapha*, Vol. II, edited by R. H. Charles.

'My son, thou hast been to me like the young swallows which fell out of their nest; and a cat caught them and said to them, "If it had not been for me, great evil would have befallen you". They answered and said to her, "Is that why thou hast put us in thy mouth?"'

There is an interesting example of what is probably a Canaanite proverb in a collection of writings known as the Amarna Letters. These are written mostly in cuneiform Babylonian script which was current in the second millennium B.C. Numerous glosses on this correspondence reveal traces of Canaanite dialect. One letter seems to be written in pure Canaanite. It was sent by a prince named Lab'ayu to his Egyptian overlord, Akhenaton, near the end of the fourteenth century B.C. The prince is anxious to defend himself against the charge that he has unlawfully used his army without first obtaining the consent of Pharaoh. He defends himself by quoting a proverbial saying: 'Further, when (even) ants are smitten, they do not accept it (passively), but they bite the hand of the man who smites them'.[1]

The Ras Shamra Tablets also are of interest. These were written about 1400 B.C., and the style of writing indicates a process of literary development over a long period, estimated by some to have been as long as four centuries.

The following utterance, which seems to have been in popular use, shows by its style a close resemblance to a type commonly found in Wisdom writings:

'Like the heart of a cow for her calf,
 Like the heart of a ewe for her lamb,
 So's the heart of Anath for Baal.'

[1] *Ancient Near Eastern Texts*, edited by J. B. Pritchard, p. 486.

The above rather brief survey of Wisdom writings found in the Ancient Near East has served the purpose of demonstrating from the extant literature how widespread Wisdom was. It shows that the literature manifested great variety, both in form and content. It includes short, pithy utterances of a popular nature, the kind of saying which seems to have existed orally before being given written form. There are also more literary types, which are the product of conscious art and show marks of a mastery of the literary craft, and which have evolved over a lengthy period of development. Also there are longer documents, where a specific subject or a group of related topics are discussed and developed, and have been written for consumption by an educated public. All kinds of subjects have come within the scope of the Wisdom writers. The one proviso seems to have been that the subject was of human interest, that it should concern man in his human situation wherever he might be and wherever he dwelt. The concerns of Everyman, Jew, Gentile or Heathen were discussed. So long as it had to do with life, a man's daily work, his domestic problems, his family, friends and employees, it was raw material for Wisdom. It might deal with illness, sorrow, destiny, or the unexpected turn of the wheel of fortune. If it was the sort of thing men talked about or pondered over, either in the silence of their own heart or with their neighbour, then sooner or later it became grist for the mill of the Wisdom writer.

When we turn to the Wisdom Literature of the Bible, we shall find that we are not dealing with some new or strange literary phenomenon. The writings which will come under our consideration will belong to a class which was well established in the life of the Ancient Near East.

III.—BIBLICAL WISDOM LITERATURE

THE central core of Wisdom Literature is the three books Job, Proverbs and Ecclesiastes. Around this there are numerous other writings which, either in form or content or both, have some right to be included in a wider definition of Wisdom Literature. These writings vary considerably in size, style of writing and subject-matter.

First, there are those popular sayings which are distilled from life's experiences. The common feature in this group is that along with sharpness of observation there is an economical use of words. Good examples of these are:

'Therefore it became a proverb, "Is Saul also among the prophets?"' (1 Sam 10:12),

'Out of the wicked comes forth wickedness' (1 Sam 24:13),

'Let not him that girds on his armour boast himself as he that puts it off' (1 Kings 20:11).

'For they sow the wind
And they reap the whirlwind' (Hos 8:7).

'Let us eat and drink,
For tomorrow we die' (Isa 22:13).

'Is there no balm in Gilead?
Is there no physician there?' (Jer 8:22).

'The fathers have eaten sour grapes, and the children's teeth are set on edge' (Ezek 18:2).

Secondly, there is a group which is slightly more literary in form. These are longer in size and are not proverbs in the same sense as the first group. Some of them might be classified as parables or allegories, others as riddles, some again as fables and there are others which have been given the technical title of 'taunt songs'. Although such titles indicate a degree of variety, yet they have enough in common to justify us in grouping them together. They usually involve a comparison between one thing and another. This is more obvious in Hebrew than in English, as in most occurrences, Hebrew uses the one term, *mashal*, to cover them all whereas English has to use parable or riddle or fable or taunt song. What they are like may be seen from the following examples:

(*a*) In Ezek 24:1–5 the prophet is commanded to utter an allegory,

'Set on the pot, set it on,
  pour in water also;
  put in it the pieces of flesh,
  all the good pieces, the thigh and the shoulder;
  fill it with choice bones.
  Take the choicest one of the flock,
  pile the logs under it;
  boil its pieces,
  seethe also its bones in it.'

(*b*) An example of the riddle is seen in the contest between Samson and his companions, where the latter say to Samson, 'Put your riddle that we may hear it', and he said to them:

'Out of the eater came something to eat,
  Out of the strong came something sweet' (Judges 14:13f).

(*c*) Perhaps the best known fable is the one told by Jotham (Judges 9:8):

'The trees once went forth to anoint a king over them;
and they said to the olive tree, "Reign over us . . .".'

It goes on to address the fig tree, the vine, and lastly the
bramble. A briefer fable occurs at 2 Kings 14:9, where
Jehoash, king of Israel replies to Amaziah, king of
Judah:

'A thistle on Lebanon sent to a cedar on Lebanon,
saying, "Give your daughter to my son for a wife; and
a wild beast of Lebanon passed by and trampled down
the thistle".'

(*d*) There are several examples of the Taunt Song, but
the outstanding one is Isa 14:4f, where the prophet
addresses the king of Babylon, although, of course, the
song may have originated in much earlier times. It is
too long to quote, but the following extracts may
indicate its quality:

'How the oppressor has ceased,
the insolent fury ceased!

.   .   .   .   .

How you are fallen from heaven,
O Day star, son of Dawn!
How you are cut down to the ground
You who laid the nations low.'

.   .   .   .   .

In the examples quoted above we have refrained from
referring to the Psalms. But there are many illustrations
of Wisdom compositions in the Psalms. The presence of
such compositions is an indication that Wisdom in Israel
was not in opposition to religion. Even where Wisdom
is, in general, characterized by a secular and humanistic
outlook, these two terms are not to be taken too nar-
rowly, nor have we to apply our modern distinctions

between sacred and secular in a rigid manner. The Psalms we are considering show that Wisdom as a way of thinking and writing was moving nearer to the cult and was not limited solely to social and political life. Just as the Psalms as a whole are greatly varied, so we find that the Wisdom psalms too show a marked variety. For our immediate purposes it will be helpful to consider these psalms in four different groups:

(*a*) *Brief Sayings*, incorporated in a psalm. A good example is the first verse of Ps 127:

'Unless the Lord builds the house,
 Those who build it labour in vain.'

and also Ps 133:1, where the didactic element is more prominent:

'Behold, how good and pleasant it is
 When brothers dwell in unity.'

(*b*) *Wisdom Poem*. In this group the Psalmist discusses a frequently recurring question such as the wise attitude to earthly possessions. This is clearly expressed in Ps 49, where the Psalmist contrasts the reliance of the wealthy on their possessions with his own reliance on God. The Wisdom vocabulary is well represented in this psalm:

'I will incline my ear to a proverb;
 I will solve my riddle to the music of the lyre' (v. 4).

Here the word 'proverb' means a divine oracle, heard by inspiration, and 'riddle' means a perplexing problem.

'Truly no man can ransom himself,
 or give to God the price of his life,
 for the ransom of his life is costly,
 and can never suffice' (vv. 7, 8).

'Man cannot abide in his pomp'
he is like the beasts that perish' (v. 20).

(c) The third group includes *Didactic Psalms*. They
contain teaching about the 'fear of God' (Ps 25) or contain admonitions to godliness based on the psalmist's
experience. Much of the language echoes the phraseology
of Wisdom Literature:

'Come, O sons, listen to me,
I will teach you the fear of the Lord (34:11).

'Men of low estate are but a breath,
men of high estate are a delusion;
in the balances they go up;
they are together lighter than a breath' (62:9).

'The fear of the Lord is the beginning of wisdom;
a good understanding have all those who practise it.
His praise endures for ever' (111:10).

Ps 37 should be included in this group and calls for
special mention. It is largely made up of disconnected
proverbs. It is written as an acrostic, in that the initial
letter of the first word in each alternate verse follows the
order of the Hebrew alphabet. The writer speaks as a
mature wise man:

'I have been young, and now am old;
yet I have not seen the righteous forsaken
or his children begging bread' (v. 25).

'The mouth of the righteous man utters wisdom,
and his tongue speaks justice' (v. 30).

'I have seen a wicked man overbearing,
and towering like a cedar of Lebanon.
Again I passed by, and, lo, he was no more;
Though I sought him, he could not be found' (vv. 35,
36).

The closeness of this psalm to Wisdom teaching receives further confirmation in that the opening verse is practically a repetition of Prov 24:19:

'Fret not yourself because of the wicked,
 be not envious of wrongdoers!'

(d) The last group has *Religious Doubt* as the subject-matter. The outstanding example is Ps 73. It describes the Psalmist's struggle to maintain faith in God in face of the prosperity of the wicked and the afflictions of the just. Although on a much smaller scale, the psalm has affinity with the Book of Job. The author paints a vivid picture of the overbearing insolence of the wicked:

'They set their mouths against the heavens,
 and their tongue struts through the earth' (v. 9).
'Behold, these are the wicked;
 always at ease, they increase in riches.
All in vain have I kept my heart clean
 and washed my hands in innocence' (vv. 12, 13).

However, despite the profit received by the wicked in this life, the Psalmist affirms that his experience of fellowship with God is richer than any material gain:

'Thou dost guide me with thy counsel
 and afterwards thou wilt receive me to glory.' (v. 24)

The above extracts show that Wisdom is much more pervasive in the Old Testament than the precise use of the term Wisdom Literature might indicate. It is true, of course, that these extracts are not presented specifically as Wisdom compositions, but are incidental parts in a narrative in the form of a proverb or parable, and in other cases, as part of a psalm. Such Wisdom writings which, from the literary point of view, seem to be almost incidental in comparison with the Wisdom compositions like Job, Proverbs and Ecclesiastes, show by their very presence in the midst of what is not technically Wisdom Literature how pervasive and acceptable Wisdom modes of thought and expression were to the Israelites. This becomes even clearer when we take note of two other manifestations of Wisdom in the Old Testament: first the 'royal' or 'kingly' Wisdom, as seen in Solomon, and secondly to the 'wise man' or 'sage' as seen in Joseph.

The tradition concerning Wisdom focuses the light on Solomon, but the Old Testament brings both David and Hezekiah into connection with Royal Wisdom. This may be regarded as evidence for the close connection between wisdom and kingship. In this, of course, Israel is only sharing in a view which was common in the Ancient Near East, for there kings were supposed to be especially endowed with Wisdom.

There are two clear statements about the wisdom imparted to David. In both cases, David is compared for Wisdom with 'the angel of God' (2 Sam 14:17, 20; 19:27). The language, of course, is the conventional formula of flattery. But that should not be allowed to obscure the fact that it is applied to David when he is about to perform a function which is particularly expected of a king, namely to make an important judicial decision. In both cases the decisions are closely connected with the throne, the one involving Absalom and the other Mephibosheth, both being related to the royal family. David has to take the responsibility of making a decision which no one but he could make. The decisions may have been forced on David but he decides rightly because he has, as the wise woman of Tekoa says, the Wisdom 'to discern good and evil' (2 Sam 14:17); indeed, he has 'wisdom like the wisdom of the angel of God' (v. 20). In the case of Mephibosheth the prince is brought before David and has to explain why he did not come to the help of David in his time of need. In the course of his self-defence, Mephibosheth says 'My lord the king is like the angel of God' (2 Sam 19:27), but he moves on to the inevitable inference from such a claim, namely 'do therefore what seems good to you'. A king with such Wisdom would be able to make the wise decision, even in difficult circumstances, and Mephibosheth was prepared to rely on it. These two incidents illustrate that the endowment of wisdom so far as the king is concerned is directed towards the kingly functions of administering justice.

It is probable that the Wisdom Solomon prayed for, and with which he was endowed, was essentially the same in principle as was manifested in David's behaviour. Solomon's desire was to be a successful ruler. If he had the ability to fulfil the royal responsibilities this would manifest itself in his power to decide between right and wrong (or the 'good and evil' spoken of by the woman of Tekoa) and thereby administer justice. The tradition is in no doubt that Solomon was endowed with wisdom. The first piece of evidence is the story about the two women, both of whom claimed to be mother of one and the same child (1 Kings 3:16–28). Doubtless the story comes from the common stock of world-wide folk-lore and is not peculiar to Solomon. But its repetition here leads up to the inevitable conclusion of the wise Solomon: 'And all Israel heard of the judgment which the King had rendered; and they stood in awe of the King, because they perceived that the wisdom of God was in him, to render justice' (v. 28). But the power of Solomon goes even further than that. He has the ability to administer the affairs of state in relation to foreign nations wisely too. For, not only did Solomon make arrangements with Hiram, king of Tyre, for the building of the temple, but the outcome of their negotiations was, 'and there was peace between Hiram and Solomon; and the two of them made a treaty' (1 Kings 5:12). Through Wisdom, Solomon exhibited both an acute mind, capable of making an immediate decision, and also skill in peaceful diplomacy. But alongside this view of Solomon's Wisdom, there emerges a view which is quite new in Israel and must now be considered.

It is additionally claimed that the Wisdom of Solomon 'surpassed the wisdom of all the people of the east, and all the wisdom of Egypt. For he was wiser than all other men . . .' (1 Kings 4:30f). In these verses reference is made to Solomon's composition of proverbs and songs, to his utterances about trees, beasts, birds, reptiles and fish. Other great claims are made on his behalf in the account of the visit of the Queen of Sheba (1 Kings 10:1–24). The opening verse sets the tone of the whole chapter, 'Now when the queen of Sheba heard of the fame of Solomon concerning the name of the Lord, she came to test him with hard questions'. The queen ends her praise with, 'Your wisdom and your prosperity surpass the report which I heard' (v. 7). The account as a whole concludes, 'Thus King Solomon excelled all the kings of the earth in riches and in wisdom. And the whole earth sought the presence of Solomon to hear his wisdom which God had put into his mind' (vv. 23, 24).

After making allowance for the exaggerated language applied to Solomon, it should be noticed that the Wisdom referred to here is rather different from the Wisdom Solomon prayed for and received and exercised. That Wisdom showed itself in his shrewd dealings with human nature and in his diplomatic skill in negotiations with Hiram. This other wisdom seems to deal with brilliant utterances, encyclopaedic knowledge of the world of nature, ability to solve riddles and answer hard questions. This Wisdom is literary and intellectual rather than practical. This 'brilliant wisdom' has formed the basis for 'Solomon and all his glory' (Matt 6:29). But Old Testament scholars believe there is much to suggest that this 'brilliant wisdom' attributed to Solomon is not based on the historical Solomon but is the work of later editors who aimed at magnifying his reputation. Although this view may subtract somewhat from the glory traditionally ascribed to Solomon personally, it does not fundamentally change the fact of the intimately close association between kingship and Wisdom. Even if, as is probable, literary Wisdom with its collections of utterances and songs, its lists of nature-phenomena, is to be set in the time of Hezekiah, it still retains the connection between the court and the Wisdom Movement. The splendour of the royal establishment was enhanced by the cultivation of Wisdom in this more sophisticated form. By this practice, Israel was simply keeping in step with the nations round about it, and in particular, it was following the established custom of what was current in the court of the Egyptians.

Further confirmation of the correctness of this view is found when we examine the connection between King Hezekiah and Wisdom. There is a curious reference to this connection at Prov 25:1, which forms the superscription to a section extending to the end of ch. 29: 'These also are proverbs of Solomon which the men of Hezekiah king of Judah copied'. The almost obvious inference from this is that Hezekiah had scribes around him who were qualified to do literary work. Hezekiah is at least a patron of literature. The verb 'copied' may here mean 'transcribed', that is, transcribed from one manuscript to another. According to 2 Kings 18:18 and 32 (cf. 19:2) Hezekiah had a staff which was expert in writing, namely 'Shebnah the secretary' and 'Joah . . . the recorder'. He also is credited with quoting a Wisdom proverbial utterance: 'Children have come to the birth, and there is no strength to bring them forth' (2 Kings 19:3). These items about Hezekiah are quite unimportant when considered by themselves, in separation from one another, but they gain in importance when we remember the historical situation. It was in this period that Hezekiah was leading Israel away from the domination of Assyria on the one hand, and on the other, moving nearer to the Egyptian way of life, especially as that might be used with advantage in his own royal court. This movement was part of an attempt to revive the national spirit within Israel, and took the form, in part at least, of refurbishing the glory which was associated with the name of Solomon. Another element in the situation at this time was the coming closer together of Israel and Judah, and it seems to be in relation to this movement that earlier records and traditions of the past of the two nations were brought up to date. There is much to support the view that in the time of Hezekiah there was an active literary movement, almost certainly centred in a scribal school, closely attached to the court, and of course, dependent on the support of the king. This kind of activity doubtless began before Hezekiah's time, but seems to have attained official status as part of the royal establishment in his reign. Hezekiah may well have aimed at drawing attention to the continuity between his aims and those of his brilliant predecessor, Solomon. Every effort he made to add to the cultural and intellectual splendour of his court would find all the readier acceptance if he could connect it with the name of Solomon, the wise king *par excellence*. What we have in Hezekiah is the culmination point in the development of one aspect of the Wisdom Movement in Israel. In his time, literary Wisdom, with its interest in nature and its concern with kingship, becomes established. Wisdom is now something wider than an interest in popular sayings; it has become didactic, and it is centred in the life of the court. Kingship and Wisdom are bound together.

The other figure which calls for consideration is that of Joseph. He has every right to be regarded as the Hebrew example of the 'wise man'. The story of Joseph[1] is didactic in aim. Its form differs from that of other Wisdom literature in being a connected, unified story rather than a collection of proverbs or a miniature essay. In its thought, too, it is distinctively Israelite in that it expresses faith in the over-ruling Wisdom of God, who in His own secret way blesses the wise man. Joseph represents the able young man who, endowed with Wisdom, attains the highest position in the land, and ultimately prospers in all he puts his hand to. In the process, which is not automatic but full of trial and effort, he suffers degradation, temptation and imprisonment. But, when the occasion demands the services of a truly wise man, Joseph emerges triumphant. Yet, even when he shows greater Wisdom than the professional wise men of Egypt, he modestly ascribes his success to God (Gen 40:8; 41:16). Joseph does more than utter wise words. He gives Pharaoh effective, practical counsel. The high point in this manifestation of Joseph's Wisdom follows the counsel he gave to Pharaoh in connection with the expected famine. This proposal seemed good to Pharaoh and to all his servants. 'Can we find such a man as this, in whom is the spirit of God?' So

---

[1] The story of Joseph circulated at an early date and in its written form is somewhat earlier than the eighth century B.C.

Pharaoh said to Joseph, 'Since God has shown you all this, there is none so discreet and wise as you are' (Gen 41:37–39). Pharaoh appoints Joseph vizier and leaves him to work out the plans to meet the coming famine. Joseph's plans are successful. Even in the midst of the famine, through Joseph's efforts Pharaoh is able to amass money, cattle, horses, flocks, herds, asses and even land (41:13f). The story of Joseph exemplifies the ideal held up before Israel in the Book of Proverbs 22:29:

> 'Do you see a man skilful in his work?
> He will stand before kings;
> he will not stand before obscure men.'

We can see in Joseph how the ideal of the wise man or sage has been integrated into the religious tradition of the Old Testament. Joseph's success was no mere lucky accident. It was the fruit of discipline and prudence. Joseph was a Hebrew, not an Egyptian, and all that he did, whether in prison or in palace, was done in the fear of the Lord. His Wisdom belonged to Israel.

In concluding this chapter it may be helpful to recapitulate the several aims it has had in view. First, an attempt has been made to show how pervasive Wisdom utterances and thoughts are in the Old Testament. Secondly, examples of the different kinds of Wisdom compositions show what varied forms Wisdom writing takes. There are popular proverbs, some short and others long. There are allegories, riddles, fables and taunt songs, and forms more commonly found among the Psalms. Thirdly, some forms of Wisdom writings take their place, almost unconsciously, within the framework of what purports to be a historical narrative. This is seen quite clearly in the accounts of the lives of kings like David, Solomon and Hezekiah. It is also seen in the story

c

of Joseph, which is a classic biography of the wise man. The discovery that there are these three different approaches to Wisdom writings in the Old Testament should help us to realize that this kind of writing has become native and indigenous to the Israelite way of thinking. For although it is true that Israel owed much to other nations in this area of its culture, and although it borrowed from the literature of other nations, the end-product is distinctively Hebrew. Although there are many universal and humanistic elements in these writings, yet they are presented in a framework which is Hebrew, and these writings with all their earthy and salty or even sophisticated Wisdom are preserved within the context of Old Testament faith.

IV.—JOB, PROVERBS AND ECCLESIASTES

THE three books which form the Wisdom Literature *par excellence* in the Old Testament are Job, Proverbs and Ecclesiastes. They are the literary precipitate of the Wisdom Movement as it found expression in Israel. The varied nature of their contents, the different styles of writing, the separare ways they came into existence are but the natural reflection of the variety and difference to be found within the Wisdom Movement itself. To illustrate this, the following generalization may be permitted. Job represents the didactic and poetic form of Wisdom; Proverbs preserves prudential teachings in the form of brief proverbs and short essays, and Ecclesiastes contains reflections and wise sayings, culled from life by the wise man as he reflected on the human situation.

The oldest of these three books, the Book of Proverbs, is fundamentally a collection of proverbs which has grown out of previous collections and has reached its present form quite slowly over a number of centuries. But its proverbs are not just popular sayings or folk-maxims. Their polished form and literary artistry demand that they be treated as the considered teaching of the wise men or sages. They include sayings of many different kinds. There are admonitions and aphorisms, observations about the world of men and nature, utterances with a religious flavour and others again which are quite secular. Whatever be the aim of the proverbs, the essential literary unit is what in Hebrew is called the *mashal.* The *mashal* takes many different forms, but its general purpose is to draw attention to some resemblances between one thing and another, or to make a comparison between them. The *mashal* was uttered with some degree of authority. It was a teaching, an instruction, or a counsel emanating from a wise man, that is, one endowed with the gift of wisdom. It was an utterance which was relevant to human conduct. It was meant to be obeyed. It was offered to the man who sought mastery over life and aimed at this end with the help of Wisdom.

The opening verse of the Book of Proverbs is the beginning of a superscription which extends to v. 6. It ascribes authorship to Solomon. The remaining verses of the superscription indicate the aim of the book. It is that men may acquire Wisdom, insight, prudence, knowledge, and how, as v. 6 expresses it,

'to understand a proverb and a figure,
the words of the wise and their riddles.'

There is no need to press the claim that Solomon is the sole author. To do so would contradict the fact that elsewhere in the book other proverbs are ascribed to other authors or collectors, such as 'the wise' (22:17), 'The words of Agur' (30:1) and 'The words of Lemuel' (31:1). The book has been issued under the authority of the name of Solomon. It may actually preserve writings which emanate from his time. This may be part justification for claiming his authorship for some of the proverbs. But the evidence seems to show that the book grew up over a period of centuries rather than years. It contains traditions and allusions which connect it with Wisdom thought and language among Canaanites and Egyptians. Nevertheless, in its present form it is a characteristic product of Hebrew Wisdom.

The book divides itself into separate sections as is indicated to some extent by the superscriptions which have been inserted here and there. It is convenient to examine it in seven parts, although others may divide it in slightly different ways.

1. *Chapters* 1–9. This is an introductory section setting forth the claims and merits of Wisdom. The proverbs take the form of longer sentences and brief poems, in distinction from the short Wisdom sentences elsewhere in the book. The nature of Wisdom itself is discussed and the idea of the personification of Wisdom is prominent. This section in its present form is regarded as the latest written part of the book. A date of the fourth or even the third century has been suggested. This late date has found support in the view that the sophisticated teaching about personified Wisdom in chs. 8 and 9, so it was asserted, demanded a date in the post-exilic period. The more recent view claims that the speculation about Wisdom is not a late phenomenon but can be traced back to Canaanite and Phoenician influences of an earlier period and to some time before the Exile. In its present form the section should perhaps be dated in the fifth century B.C., with elements which go back to an earlier age.

The contents are presented in the style of a Wisdom teacher addressing his pupils in the 'wisdom school'. He speaks like a father addressing his son,

'Hear, my son, your father's instruction . . .' (1:8)

The formula, 'my son' occurs frequently. It is a conventional phrase and is used by a teacher to his pupils. It is found, too, in Babylonian and Egyptian wisdom. It should be remembered that in Hebrew the verb 'hear' can have the significance of 'obey'. The essence of the teaching in this section is expressed in 1:7, thus:

'The fear of the Lord is the beginning of knowledge;
fools despise wisdom and instruction.'

2. *Chapters* 10:1–22:16. This section has a brief super-scription, 'The proverbs of Solomon'. It is the oldest section and also the longest, containing some 375 proverbs. These are short, being only one line long in Hebrew and divided into two parts (19:7 is an exception). There is normally some connection between the two parts of the proverb. It may be, firstly, on the basis of resemblance:

'Condemnation is ready for scoffers
and flogging for the backs of fools' (19:29).

This kind of resemblance is called *synonymous parallelism*, and is indicated here by the terms 'condemnation' and 'flogging', and 'scoffers' and 'fools'. The second kind of connection is called *antithetic parallelism*, and is based on the difference between the first and second part of the proverb, thus:

'A false balance is an abomination to the Lord,
but a just weight is his delight' (11:1).

The third kind is called *synthetic parallelism*; here the second part completes the thought of the first, thus:

'Like a gold ring in a swine's snout
is a beautiful woman without discretion' (11:22).

The proverbs in this section are objective statements of fact. The hearer is not exhorted or challenged. But it is presumed he will be amenable to the teaching implicit in the proverb. But these proverbs are not entirely secular. God is, as it were, the implicit assumption of the wise man. That is why references to what is an abomination to the Lord, or to His love for righteousness fit in so naturally to what otherwise appears to be a secular observation.

3. *Chapters 22:17–24:22, and 24:23–34.* This third section is in two parts. (It is possible that the second part is an independent section.) The first part refers to its contents as 'the words of the wise' (22:17) and the second has the superscription, 'These also are sayings of the wise' (24:23).

A characteristic of this section is that it is made up of brief poems of four or more lines, instead of short proverbs. Another feature is that the wise man addresses his hearer directly—'Incline your ear', 'apply your mind', 'to you, even to you'—instead of objectively as in the previous section.

The first part has very close connections with the Egyptian text known as 'The Instruction of Amen-Em-Opet'. The literary relation between the Egyptian writing and this part has already been discussed in the chapter on Egyptian Wisdom. This part is a good example of how Hebrew didactic Wisdom appropriated for itself writings first composed elsewhere. It aims at providing instruction for young men preparing to equip themselves for office in the affairs of state, and also for success in life in the larger world. It begins with a call to hearken to instruction. The teaching which follows is varied and comprehensive, rather than logically systematic. It deals with such topics as choice of companions, treatment of the poor, hot-tempered men, surety for pledges, table-etiquette, material wealth, gluttony, filial piety, bad women, and drunkenness. It also deals with the advantages of Wisdom, the need of perseverance, and concludes with an exhortation to 'fear the Lord and the king'.

The second part begins with a warning against

partiality in judging. It continues with advice about maintaining a family and concludes with a shrewd, humorous poem on the danger which besets the sluggard.

As already noted, Egyptian and probably other foreign influences have helped to determine both the contents and the form of this section. But this does not mean that there has been mere plagiarism. Alongside the literary appropriation of material originating outside Israel, the section as a whole contains hints, allusions and assumptions which are in harmony with the religious point of view of the Old Testament.

4. *Chapters* 25–29. This section has the superscription, 'These also are proverbs of Solomon which the men of Hezekiah king of Judah copied'. The mention of Solomon's name may be testimony in support of the view that in the time of Hezekiah, a revival of interest in Wisdom Literature led both to the preservation in writing of proverbs coming from the time of Solomon, and to the composition of new Wisdom writings. Many different kinds of proverbs are found in this section, including the different kinds of parallelism. An example of antithetic parallelism at 25:2 is:

'It is the glory of God to conceal things,
  but the glory of kings is to search things out.'

All manner of subjects are treated, but, in general, the tone is secular and objective. But this does not exclude elements which can be described as humane and charitable. Among the rather prosaic proverbs in this section, one stands out in virtue of its intrinsic qualities:

'If your enemy is hungry, give him bread to eat;
  and if he is thirsty, give him water to drink' (25:21).

It is interesting that the second line in the following verse supplies a utilitarian motive as an inducement,

'and the Lord will reward you' (25:22).

Some slight differences in form can be discerned within this section to the extent that in chs. 25–27, the literary unit tends to be longer than in chs. 28–29. The former group prefers proverbs based on resemblances:

'A man without self-control
is like a city broken into and left without walls'
(25:28),

whereas the latter prefers those which show differences:

'The wicked flee when no one pursues,
but the righteous are as bold as a lion' (28:1).

The chief topics discussed are good manners, the fool, the sluggard and the tongue. There are also numerous disconnected popular proverbs.

5. *Chapter* 30. This section has the superscription, 'The words of Agur son of Jakeh of Massa'. It seems to be in two parts, vv. 1–14, and 15–33. Nothing is known of Agur and Jakeh and it is improbable that the names are Israelite. Possibly 'Massa' is not a name and it can mean 'oracle'. The contents of the first part are in keeping with teaching found elsewhere in the Old Testament. Indeed, vv. 3 and 4 recall parts of Isaiah and Job. Although vv. 7–14 are secular in tone, yet the point of view expressed in them has affinities with some of the teaching in the Book of Psalms.

The second part, vv. 15–33, is noteworthy for its numerical proverbs. The characteristic feature is to refer

to the number 'three' in the first line and to number
'four' in the second, thus:

'Three things are never satisfied;
four never say, "Enough":' (30:15).

The other examples are at vv. 18, 21 and 29. The example
at v. 24 differs in that the 'three' is not mentioned, but
only the 'four':

'Four things on earth are small'.

It is conjectured that behind the numerical proverb there
was originally a riddle, such as, 'What four things
etc. . . .?'

6. *Chapter* 31:1–9. The superscription reads, 'The
words of Lemuel, king of Massa, which his mother taught
him'. Lemuel is an unknown king and Massa is in North-
West Arabia. It is exceptional for the mother to be mentioned in a context like this, as instruction to a son is
usually connected with the king. The instruction is
prudential in character. The king is warned against bad
women and wine. He is exhorted to render justice to the
needy. The instruction fits into the pattern of Wisdom
teaching offered to kings in the Ancient Near East.

7. *Chapter* 31:10–31. This has the form of an acrostic
poem, written in the order of the Hebrew alphabet,
about a virtuous wife. It is possible it may have been
composed to set an ideal before young women of marriage-
able age. In the poem, the wife reigns supreme in the
domestic sphere and she is inspired by the motive of
bringing honour to the name of her husband. In v. 26
reference is made to her Wisdom and her teaching. It is
a noteworthy feature that the Book of Proverbs should
close with a reference to the wise and virtuous housewife,
and that she can be cited as an example of Wisdom.

True to the fundamental thesis of the book as a whole, it is pointed out (v. 30) that the fear of the Lord is found in her.

The Book of Job

The Book of Job easily divides itself into five parts:

1. *Chapters 1 and 2.* These form the Prologue and are written in prose.

2. *Chapters 3–31.* This is the main poem and is made up of the speeches of Job and his three friends.

3. *Chapters 32–37.* This is a poem, added at a later date, and ascribed to another speaker, not previously mentioned, Elihu.

4. *Chapters 38:1–42:6.* The Divine Speech.

5. *Chapter 42:7–17.* The epilogue, written in prose.

The central human figure is Job and we are told how he behaved in good fortune and bad. This interest in human behaviour under adversity is a subject commonly dealt with in Wisdom Literature. Job's claim to integrity, made on his behalf by God, is put to the test. We are shown how an innocent man is outrageously mishandled in life and misjudged by friends. The current Wisdom theology should have been able to give an explanation of the desperate plight of Job, but it fails to do so. Under the pressure of his sufferings he repudiates the conventional orthodoxy which sought to explain the Divine Governance of the world on the basis of a theory of retribution. The argument of the central core of the book (chs. 3–31) is conducted in the style of a dispute among the Wise Men. Job and his friends speak as teachers of Wisdom. The friends represent conventional Wisdom teaching, although, of course, there are minor differences in emphasis among them. Although Job, too, is to be regarded as a 'Wisdom teacher', he rejects the current theology and refutes the points of view of his friends. But even Job himself found no satisfactory answer to his problem. Nor can it be said that the later poem of Elihu (chs. 32–37) solves the problem. The book ends with the vindication of Job's character (rather than his teaching), the condemnation of the teaching of his friends, and the renewal of his prosperity.

In a book of such length, with so many speakers, and expressing different views, it is not surprising that there are several ideas about wisdom. There is, first, the popular Wisdom which expresses itself in brief proverbs:

'As I have seen, those who plough iniquity
 and sow trouble reap the same' (4:8).

'Surely vexation kills the fool,
 and jealousy slays the simple' (5:2).

'Can papyrus grow where there is no marsh?
 Can reeds flourish where there is no water?' (8:11).

'Wisdom is with the aged
 and understanding in length of days' (12:2).

Secondly, Wisdom is sometimes used to indicate human skill and ingenuity. This kind of Wisdom is found frequently throughout the Old Testament. In Job it finds most brilliant expression in the first eleven verses of ch. 28. There the technical ability of man is described in terms of mining operations. There is an uninhibited appreciation of man's capacity to contend with a recalcitrant nature, as seen in rock, in flood-water, in darkness and in his taking over of inaccessible sites.

The third kind of Wisdom is specialized, in that it is attributed exclusively and uniquely to God, and denied totally to man. This Wisdom is treated in ch. 28:12–27. It has manifested itself as that Wisdom which was associated with God in creation (vv. 23–27).

In addition to these different ideas about what Wisdom is, the book provides an example of how a group of Wisdom thinkers dealt with an important human problem. By means of the arguments of Job and his friends and by means of the later insertion of Elihu's speech, we are shown, as it were, Wisdom thinking in progress. Different points of view are expressed one after the other. Direct answers are hardly ever given, for the replies tend to be counter-views or complementary views, rather than answers. Even although there is hardly any discernible progress in the argument, to judge by the standards of Western logic, nevertheless the deep struggle of the human soul to gain some understanding of the bewildering problem is laid open before the reader. It may be that Job represents a small minority of thinkers within the Wisdom Movement, and he may even be, on occasion, in a minority of one. His friends, too, may represent the current conventional theology of the Wisdom Movement. Elihu, on the other hand, may represent another group, who had to argue against two points of view. That is, they repudiated the unorthodox teaching of Job, and also they sought to re-adapt the conventional teaching of the friends in order that it could deal adequately with the kind of problem which confronted Job. But it cannot be claimed that Elihu's teaching was any more successful than that of the others. As a whole, the book shows the Wisdom teaching undergoing an internal re-appraisal of some of its own principles. Job breaks free from his contemporaries, and even from his successors, but he is still a Wisdom teacher, and indeed, the greatest of them all.

Brief allusion has already been made to the different kinds of Wisdom envisaged in the book, and in particular to ch. 28. A no less interesting feature about Wisdom, in a more literary aspect is found in the Divine Speech which begins at ch. 38. The speech resembles a controversy somewhat in the style of what might obtain in a law court. It consists of question and answer, in a brilliant style. Questions are hurled at Job and he has no answer to them. The divine power manifest in the world of nature is set before him, in a style which has affinities with Ps 148, which itself is a hymn to God wherein the whole created world is called upon to praise His name. A characteristic of ch. 38f is the detailed reference to the varied phenomena of the natural world. The several items cited resemble an encyclopaedic list of the marvels of nature, cosmological, meteorological, biological, zoological and so forth. This style of writing was probably derived from conventional, stereotyped lists commonly found in Egyptian literature. Such lists—slight and tentative beginnings of a scientific interest in nature as known to Israel—may lie behind the reference in 1 Kings 4:33 to Solomon's Wisdom, where it is claimed, 'He spoke of trees, from the cedar that is in Lebanon to the hyssop that grows out of the wall; he spoke also of beasts, and of birds, and of reptiles, and of fish'.

A work so rich and varied as Job is not easily classified, but it can be claimed that it has no rival as the supreme product of the Wisdom Literature.

Ecclesiastes

The intriguing title of the book may be a *nom-de-plume*, or possibly not a proper name at all, but a designation for an official who addresses an assembly. The claim that the author is King Solomon (1:12) is hardly more than a fiction. The ascription to Solomon may have been a help in getting so heterodox a work into the canon. From quite an early point in its history its right to be accepted as scripture was contested. A Talmudic saying states that both its beginning and ending are religious, but even this apologia suggests some degree of opposition to its inclusion in the canon. The probability is that it is a product of the Wisdom Movement in Israel some time in the second half of the third century B.C.

Like the other Wisdom writings it contains examples of different styles of composition. There is both prose and poetry. There are simple short proverbs:

'A good name is better than precious ointment' (7:1).

There are also warnings:

'Woe to you, O land, when your king is a child,
 and your princes feast in the morning!' (10:16),

and also beatitudes:

'Happy are you, O land, when your king is the son of free men,
 and your princes feast at the proper time' (10:17).

There are larger compositions as at 5:25, in prose:

'Be not rash with your mouth, nor let your heart be hasty to utter a word before God, for God is in heaven, and you upon earth; therefore let your words be few.'

Also, there are admonitions in interrogative form:

'Be not righteous overmuch, and do not make yourself overwise; why should you destroy yourself?' (7:16).

There are examples of parallelism in verse. An example of the synonymous type is:

'What is crooked cannot be made straight,
 and what is lacking cannot be numbered' (1:15),

and of the antithetic, in prose:

'The wise man has his eyes in his head, but the fool walks in darkness' (2:14), and of the synthetic:

'If the serpent bites before it is charmed,
 There is no advantage in a charmer' (10:11).

What can be regarded as a miniature essay is found in
the comparison between the wise youth and the foolish
king (4:13–16, 9:13–16). There is also a type of composition which is rather like an allegory. It begins at 12:3,
with—'in the day when the keepers of the house tremble'
and ends with—'or the wheel broken at the cistern'
(12:6). This is taken by many to be an allegory of the
human body in old age.

Ecclesiastes has many resemblances in style and content to Job, Proverbs and some Psalms. There is every
reason to accept the view that the book is a native
growth, produced out of the soil of Hebrew Wisdom,
despite the fact that there may be some elements in it
which seem to be opposed to the more orthodox teaching
of the Old Testament. Yet in important ways Ecclesiastes
differs from the other Wisdom writings. One marked
difference is seen if it is compared with the Book of Job.
There is an affinity between the two works in that they
both present a challenge to the current orthodoxy even
within the Wisdom Movement. It could be said of Job
that he represents the religious man engaged with his
whole being in an attempt to wrest an answer from God,
whereas Ecclesiastes turns his problem over and over
within his mind and hardly breaks out of the circle of
the earthly scene.

The strangely attractive allusive style of Ecclesiastes
makes it difficult both to analyse the form of the book
and to summarize its teaching. Some have tried to
analyse the book into three or even four parts. But it is
difficult to obtain agreement on this, largely because

there is no universal agreement as to the extent of interpolations there may be in the work. A useful way of
approaching the book as we have it today is to imagine
that Ecclesiastes is engaged in a discussion with a typical
representative of the orthodox Wisdom school. The book
can then be read as a protest against the facile optimism
which characterized many Wisdom teachers. Their
teaching had tended to concentrate on the accepted
views of popular morality as that had accumulated from
the past, and was less concerned with criticizing its own
teaching or the presuppositions which lay behind it.
Wisdom writers had produced lists or catalogues of the
phenomena men had observed in the natural world and
had noted unusual features in the created order. There
is a hint of such activities in 1 Kings 4:33, where it is
said that Solomon spoke about trees, beasts, birds, reptiles and fish. Also, these writers provided instruction for
young men who were ambitious to get on in life. Thus
they paid attention to such matters as rules for success,
riches, self-control, diligence, laziness. They dealt with
topics like behaviour at court, or in the house of the rich,
or in the presence of women, or friends, or relations.
They gave advice about executing a confidential com-
mission, or how to behave towards God, or about the
kind of conduct which brings material reward. Implicit
within this kind of teaching was the presupposition that
there was a more or less fixed order in the world, with
which a properly instructed man could come to terms for
his own advantage. It was an order which seemed to have
God for its guarantor. This order in its working out, so
it was implied, exhibited the principle of retribution and,
generally speaking, distributed rewards to the righteous
and punishment to the wicked. Such an outlook, of
course, is optimistic, and man was encouraged to believe

that if he ordered his life in accordance with wisdom, he would be able to steer clear of the dangers which would otherwise bring shipwreck to his life. The fear of God leads to success in life. Ecclesiastes does not agree with this teaching. Apart from its optimism about the relation between righteousness and prosperity, he exposes the superficiality of its teaching about God. Ecclesiastes is acutely, indeed painfully, aware of unfathomable depths in the Divine Purpose. Indeed that is part of the problem of the book. He is daunted by the width of the unbridgeable gap between God and man. He cannot find out what God has done from the beginning to the end (3:11), and, 'for God is in heaven, and you upon earth . . .' (5:2).

As already indicated, there are interpolations in the book, and some parts have been edited at a later date to make the book appear more orthodox in its teaching. These factors result in inconsistencies in the thought of the book. But there is no need to postulate direct, non-Jewish influences, especially from a Greek source. It is true there is a strong streak of pessimism in the book. But this is not necessarily due to influences from outside Israel's experience. One has only to remember that pessimism was a common mood in the third century b.c. around the Mediterranean world, and indeed elsewhere. But the earlier history of Israel shows acquaintance with a pessimistic view about life. The primeval history of Genesis, chs. 1–11, especially in chs. 2, 3 and 6, are examples of that mood. One need mention only the Serpent, the Fall, the Tower of Babel and the Flood.

The value of Ecclesiastes lies in the way the author attempts to deal with the problems which afflicted men in his day. The question, put very briefly, was, how ought men to behave in a world where the individual was helpless and the wise man suffered no better fate than the fool? Ecclesiastes doubts if man can win any worthwhile reward for all his efforts in life. God is too far above man to make any practical difference in man's lot on earth. In the long run the wise man and the fool are brought to an unfinished and unsatisfactory end by death. Ecclesiastes seems to cast doubt on the value of wisdom but on the whole he thinks the wise man is better than the fool. Nevertheless, one should not aim at being over-wise nor over-religious. Life is much too unpredictable. Chance and accident befall man without any relation to desert. Wisdom has, possibly, a relative value for life but it does not enable a man to solve the riddles of life. At the best there are some pleasures a man might enjoy in the time God allows to him. Man's lot falls in accordance with God's unknowable purpose; otherwise, all is vanity.

Ecclesiastes represents an important element in Wisdom in that he takes the spirit of enquiry just about as far as it could go. He differs from his contemporaries in that he bases his conclusions on his own keen powers of observation rather than on traditional authority. He looks upon the human scene through his own highly developed powers of introspection, and with a restraint based upon truth enunciates his sombre reflections. It is difficult, if not impossible, to know what he really believed about God. It is true that he is aware of the reality of God but he seems to place the Divine Presence far away in the dark background of life. Somehow or other, despite his great gifts and his tender sympathy with man and beast, he has been daunted in his own spirit. His God is so far away from man that it is all but impossible to have a vital, personal relationship with Him. To the extent that this was true of Ecclesiastes, it was all but inevitable that he should conclude, all is vanity.

V.—WISDOM IN THE APOCRYPHA AND PSEUDEPIGRAPHA

WISDOM Literature is representated in the Apocrypha by Ecclesiasticus and the Wisdom of Solomon. These two works continue the Wisdom tradition of the Old Testament and, in a sense, bring that tradition to the end of its development. Outside the Apocrypha, other smaller writings having a slight connection with Wisdom teaching call for mention. They are Fourth Maccabees, Pirke Aboth and the Story of Ahikar. They are contained in the Pseudepigrapha. We shall begin with the Apocrypha.

I. *Ecclesiasticus*

This book is known under two names, Ecclesiasticus, or the Wisdom of Jesus the Son of Sirach. Its second title is taken from the name of the author. He was a Jew, and composed his book in Jerusalem about 180 B.C. It was translated by his grandson, whose name is unknown, from the Hebrew into Greek, in 130 B.C. at Alexandria.

Ecclesiasticus shows the influence of the Book of Proverbs, even to the extent of containing many examples of popular proverbs:

'Happy is the husband of a good wife;
the number of his days will be doubled' (26:1).

In addition, there is an interesting literary development in what can be described as an expanded proverb.

Chapter 38:24 provides a good example:

> 'The wisdom of the scribe depends on the opportunity
> of leisure:
> 'and he who has little business may become wise.'

In this form, this proverb is probably an utterance of a
wise man. But in the hands of ben Sira, this simple proverb undergoes expansion. Starting off with praise of the
scribe and by pointing to the necessity of leisure for the
cultivation of Wisdom, it moves on to a triumphant
conclusion at 39:11:

> 'if he lives long, he will leave a name greater than a
> thousand,
> and if he goes to rest, it is enough for him.'

That is, his reputation will live on after his death. The
simple proverb has become a short essay and the wise
man has become a scribe. This assimilation of the wise
man into a scribe is a characteristic feature of Ecclesiasticus.

In its literary shape, Ecclesiasticus possesses features
which recall the style of the Book of Proverbs, in that it
frequently moves without logical transition from one
subject to another. It is, too, much longer in size than
the Wisdom of Solomon and deals with a greater number
of topics. Yet, although it is rather discursive and subject
to sudden transitions, the author writes now and then
with considerable skill. He is especially happy when describing nature in its different moods. The passage
dealing with the snowstorm, the ice, frost, wind, with his
metaphors of birds in flight, reaches high levels in poetry
(ch. 43). His celebrated panegyric, beginning (ch. 44)

'Let us now praise famous men',

has an established place in the culture of our Western civilization. He can also write in a popular way about doctors, apportioning both praise and blame. His observations about the evils of a bad wife and the blessings of a good one are shrewd and humorous. Obviously the author is a man of wide and generous sympathies. He is able to incorporate in a relatively serious work the simple human concerns of the ordinary man. He takes up a number of the themes which belong to the Wisdom teaching as it found earlier expression in the Book of Proverbs. So much so, that in his own specific instructions on proper social etiquette when dining at the table of a rich man, he renews a theme frequently treated by the wise men both in Israel and other lands.

When we examine his teaching on Wisdom, we see that he bases himself on a fairly orthodox Jewish faith. He takes the Judaism of his own day for granted and feels no need to explain it in detail nor to defend it against possible criticism. His theology leans towards the point of view which, at a later date, was commonly held by Sadducees. Like them, he has no belief in an after-life. But he evinces a deep interest in and a detailed knowledge of the temple, and in particular, of the priesthood and its ritual. When we take account of the subjects in which he is really interested—such things as Wisdom, the Law, the past history of Israel, the long line of patriarchs, famous men, heroes and heroines of the faith—it is not really surprising that he shows no deep and direct influence of Greek thought. His thinking was cast in the current moulds of Judaism. But this Judaistic element in his thought is not to be dismissed as mere conservatism; it has a positive significance. His fondness for things Jewish really indicates that he himself represents a development of thought current in his day within

Judaism itself. For our particular purpose, and with special reference to the Wisdom element in its teaching, Ecclesiasticus shows how the Wisdom Movement as a whole had moved away from the position it occupied in earlier centuries. In its earlier days, even within Israel, the interests of Wisdom were broadly human and international. But in this later period, these interests have become more national, and more institutionally religious. Wisdom shows an attitude to life which is more closely related to distinctively Jewish religious beliefs and practices. For example, at ch. 38:24, previously quoted, the figure of the wise man, traditionally a cosmopolitan figure, now wears the robes of a Jewish scribe. Related to this change, we have to note that where, traditionally, Wisdom had been understood to mean 'the fear of the Lord', it has now come to mean 'the fulfilment of the law' (19:20). Indeed, Ecclesiasticus goes so far as to identify Wisdom with the Law (24:23):

'All this is the book of the covenant of the Most High God, the law which Moses commanded as an inheritance for the congregations of Jacob.'

Doubtless he sees Wisdom through the spectacles of his Judaism, but at the same time, he admits that there is an element in Wisdom which goes beyond the frontiers of the national religion. Because of this broad-mindedness on his part, there is sometimes in his teaching what might appear to be an inconsistency. It looks like a tension between universalism and particularism. For example, at 1:9, 10, we read:

9. 'The Lord himself created wisdom;
he saw her and apportioned her,
he poured her out upon all his works.

10. She dwells with all flesh according to his gift, and
he supplied her to those who love him.'

The Wisdom created by God has been given to 'all flesh'
in that amount which God thought fit and proper, but
it was given without measure to 'those who love him',
i.e. the Jews. A similar point of view is expressed in
ch. 24. This is the great hymn wherein Wisdom praises
herself and calls attention to her virtues and functions.
Wisdom comes from God and pervades the creation. She
is present,

'in the whole earth,
and in every people and nation I have gotten a
possession.'

Yet, along with this emphasis upon the universalism
there is also the claim of a particularism:

'Make your dwelling in Jacob,
and in Israel receive your inheritance',

and in the same section (vv. 10, 11):

'In the holy tabernacle I ministered before him,
and I was established in Zion.
In the beloved city likewise he gave me a resting place,
and in Jerusalem was my dominion.'

This way of presenting the relation of Wisdom to mankind in general on the one hand and to Israel in particular
on the other may possibly owe something to the influence
of popular philosophy, such as was current amongst
Stoics. There was a tendency at work among Hellenistic
thinkers which claimed that the educated individual
shared, through his personal possession of reason, in a
universal reason which pervaded the cosmos. It may
possibly be the case that this view of the relation be-

tween Wisdom as offered to the nations and Wisdom as possessed by Jews bears a family resemblance to the teaching about the Logos in the Prologue to John's Gospel, where we are told that the Logos which enlightens all mankind nevertheless resides in a unique and distinctive way in Jesus. But whatever may have been the influences at work on the thought of Ecclesiasticus, it should be borne in mind that he was proferring to his contemporaries a practical solution of the problem of Judaism against the encroachments of Hellenism. We must not, as it were, over-theologize his writings. He seems to have been concerned about two elements in Wisdom and he sought to be just and fair towards both. First, Wisdom really was God's gift to all mankind, yet, no less truly—or should it be even more truly?—Wisdom had a unique and distinctive role to play in the destiny of Israel. Secondly, he regarded the relation between Wisdom and Israel as a privilege bestowed upon Israel by God, in order to confer blessing upon the larger world:

'I have not laboured for myself alone,
  but for all who seek instruction' (24:34).

When we take account of the changes and developments in Wisdom as portrayed by Ecclesiasticus, it becomes understandable why it is well-nigh impossible to be precise about its meaning. At one level, Wisdom is treated as a literary phenomenon, dealing with proverbs and wise utterances. Yet, even on this level, there is development. For what before was hardly more than a pithy sentence with a sharp or even salty point, becomes quite a polished essay several verses in length. Then, too, the Wise Man who formerly was quite an established institution becomes united with the scribe and as a scribe has the responsibility of preserving and teaching Wisdom. Also, the phenomenon of Wisdom, formerly universal and international in its appeal, becomes increasingly national and Jewish. Further, that Wisdom which was based on the fear of the Lord becomes, in a more precise manner, the fulfilment of the Law. But there are also important theological changes. At an earlier stage Wisdom was thought of as a divine attribute, operating rather like a mental process, as it were, inside God. But in this later period, Wisdom is externalized; it expresses something 'outside' God. Without attempting to be precise, it may be said that Wisdom has a degree of subsistence. At this stage, we may see hints of resemblance to modes of thought found in some of the more theological writings in the Bible. For example, terms like 'spirit' and 'word' in the first chapter of Genesis seem to belong to the same theological outlook. Also, what might be referred to as the feminine traits of Wisdom become clearer. Wisdom, as seen first in Proverbs ch. 7, warns young men against foreign women, and secondly, in ch. 9, where more positively Wisdom is likened to a hostess inviting her guests to enjoy the good things of her table. But when we come to the times of Ecclesiasticus (ch. 15:1–8), this feminine element is taken a step further. Here Wisdom is described as a mother, and as a wife, who will bring honour to the man who fears the Lord.

II. *The Wisdom of Solomon*

The Wisdom of Solomon seeks to combine the piety of orthodox Judaism with a popular version of Greek philosophy as these were understood in Alexandria round about the end of the first century B.C. It is the sole literary representative from Alexandria, as distinct from

Jerusalem, of a Wisdom writing. The date of writing is some time between 100 B.C. and A.D. 40. It reads like a popular, theological treatise. This view receives some support from certain references from 6:21 onwards, where the speaker, using the first person singular, seems to be speaking in the name of Solomon. But this suggestion of royal authorship is a conventional fiction, and the work is to be regarded as anonymous. It opens with an exhortation to rulers to hearken to the claims of Wisdom:

'Love righteousness, you rulers of the earth.'

The author continues with an enumeration of the conditions necessary for the acquisition of Wisdom. By beginning with this invocation to royalty, the author sets his book within that tradition which closely connects Wisdom and kingship.

The book may be divided into three sections as follows: chs. 1–5; 6–9; and 10–19. The first treats of Wisdom in its humbler and more practical uses, the second is marked by a magnificent description of the praiseworthy virtues of Wisdom, while the third draws what might be called a moral; that is, it shows how Wisdom brings blessing to the faithful and punishment to those who neglect it. The author makes extensive use of the history of Israel to point his moral, especially in this third section. But he uses history for purposes of edification rather than for accurate recording of the past. A similar point of view shows itself in his treatment of current ideas. He seems to possess at least a nodding acquaintance with, even if not a technical knowledge of, the more intellectual ideas current in his day. His philosophical vocabulary shows traces both of popular Platonism and Stoicism. If we consider even a few examples only, we shall see that he follows Plato in his belief in the pre-existence of the soul. At 8:19 he writes:

> 'As a child I was by nature well-endowed,
> and a good soul fell to my lot;
> or rather, being good, I entered an undefiled body.'

Also, he seems to accept the view that creation was made from some pre-existing matter. He writes,

> 'For thy all-powerful hand,
> which created the world out of formless matter' (11:17).

The phrase 'formless matter' fits in with a Greek view in contrast with the Old Testament view, which teaches creation out of nothing, as depicted in Genesis 1. It is probable that the author was showing deference to Greek opinion, but he was not completely consistent on this point. For at 9:1 he speaks of creation by God's word, which, of course, is nearer to the Hebrew view. Perhaps it is unfair to expect the author to be consistent and simple on such a difficult subject.

So far as Stoic influences appear to be present, he shows familiarity with its popular terminology. At 8:7, he cites the four virtues approved by Stoics, and attributes them to the power of Wisdom:

> 'For she teaches self-control and prudence, justice and courage;
> nothing in life is more profitable for men than these.'

At 1:7 he speaks of Wisdom as holding all things together and thereby giving a wholeness to creation,

> 'and that which holds all things together knows what is said.'

Perhaps most interesting of all is his use of the literary device known as *sorites*, at 6:17–20:

17. 'The beginning of wisdom is the most sincere desire for instruction,
    and concern for instruction is love of her,

18. and love of her is the keeping of her laws,
    and giving heed to her laws is assurance of immortality,

19. and immortality brings one near to God;

20. so the desire for wisdom leads to a kingdom.'

It will be seen that each successive line is linked to the preceding one by a key-word. The key-word is repeated in each pair. For example, 'instruction' in the first and second lines of v. 17, and similarly, 'laws' in v. 18. This technical device conveys the impression that a logical process is being followed out to its inevitable conclusion as expressed in v. 20. That is, love of wisdom leads to immortality, nearness to God and to a kingdom. This style of writing, of linking words in a kind of chain, was popular with Stoic writers.

However, elements such as these noted above must not be given an exaggerated importance. They are to be noted, but their significance is superficial. The author is neither a Platonist nor a Stoic. Fundamentally, he is a Jew; he believes in Israel and that his people are of special concern to God. Throughout his book he is seeking to commend Hebrew Wisdom to the learned, Gentile world as he knew it in Alexandria.

We have now to ask, what is the nature of the Wisdom recommended in this book? A direct way of answering this question is to examine the words used by our author himself at 7:22–8:1. He provides a detailed account of the many, varied characteristics of Wisdom; he cites 21 in all:

22. 'For in her there is a spirit that is intelligent, holy,
    unique, manifold, subtle,
    mobile, clear, unpolluted,
    distinct, invulnerable, loving the good, keen,
    irresistible,
23. beneficent, humane,
    steadfast, sure, free from anxiety,
    all-powerful, overseeing all,
    and penetrating through all spirits
    that are intelligent and pure and most subtle.'

The author has accumulated a large number of epithets current in theological circles. The total of twenty-one is probably intentional, in that it is the product of two sacred numbers, three and seven, thereby claiming for Wisdom that she is divine and complete. Within the limitations of a popular writing, the author has attempted to describe what he believes is the status of Wisdom, and he places it nearer to God than to man. He goes as near as thought can go, in setting Wisdom in such close proximity to God. But, as a loyal Jew, he stops short of calling Wisdom, God. He regards Wisdom as divine, and, in accordance with the gender of the word, both in Hebrew and Greek, treats it (or her) as feminine. She is at one with God and receives from Him all her gifts and graces which mark her out as unique. Although Wisdom is not a person in the (modern) sense of an independent self and agent, she is regarded as personal. She is not absolutely separate and independent from God, nor is she an equal power alongside Him. She is more like an adjective which has no value apart from the noun it is related to. She draws her existence, in all its peculiarity, from God and acts, in all ways, in complete accordance with His mind, of which she has a unique understanding. To quote the description at 7:25, 26, where she is said to emanate from God:

'For she is a breath of the power of God,
and a pure emanation of the glory of the Almighty;
therefore nothing defiled gains entrance into her.
For she is a reflection of eternal light,
a spotless mirror of the working of God,
and an image of His goodness.'

Wisdom renews all things; makes holy people into friends of God. She is beautiful, brighter than any created light such as the sun or stars, never grows dim, and enlightens man on his way through the world. Wisdom is invincible and not even evil can prevail against her (7:30). The whole wide world, from end to end, is governed and ordered by Wisdom (8:1).

So subtle and elusive a conception of Wisdom hardly permits of precise formulation. It is doubtful, too, if the many questions which naturally arise in the modern mind about Wisdom can be satisfactorily answered. This stricture needs to be borne in mind when we are tempted to analyse Wisdom in the light of our modern ideas about the self and personality. The concepts we use today have been refined by means of philosophical and psychological discussions over the centuries. By contrast, our author has been speaking from within the framework of a Judaism of two thousand years ago. His chief aim was to commend to Gentiles that Hebrew Wisdom which was God's own gift to Israel. His references to the status of Wisdom are subordinate and allusive; they are instrumental to his purpose of showing the practical importance of Wisdom in life. Nevertheless even in his brief treatment of Wisdom, the author has expressed an important truth, viz. how intimate and, indeed, unique, is the relation between Wisdom and God. It is through man's response to Wisdom that his knowledge of God is made real.

Whatever may be the final verdict on the conception of Wisdom represented in the Apocrypha, there is ample evidence to suggest that in the time span covered by Ecclesiasticus and the Wisdom of Solomon, there was a vitality and a continuity in the Wisdom Movement. These two works were called forth by the need to meet a danger which threatened to disrupt Judaism. The writers themselves were exposed to the new and attractive ideas which were part of the Hellenism around them. Naturally enough, they accepted some elements and rejected others. Each in his own way sought to present Wisdom to his contemporaries. Both believed that Wisdom, under God, belongs to Israel, and that the task of Israel is to make this Wisdom available for the whole world. It may well be that they fulfilled their task in a manner more satisfactory than they had ever hoped.

III.—*The Pseudepigrapha*

There is a sense in which it can be said that, so far as literature is concerned, Wisdom Literature reaches its terminus in the Apocrypha, and in particular in the Wisdom of Solomon. As a result of a movement which had been in process over many centuries, and which owed much to influences outside of Israel, Judaism has now created for itself a literature which is classical and normative for its faith. This corpus of Wisdom Literature, canonical and apocryphal, is sufficient for Judaism. There is no religious or moral need for more. In a sense, therefore, we have covered all that might be called Wisdom Literature in our previous pages. But, as we all know, history is never so tidy and so exact as that. For although the Apocrypha provides a useful terminus for Wisdom Literature, nevertheless there are occasional writings which have some slight connections with the Wisdom Movement, and which should be considered in the interests of completeness, even if we have to confess that they make no significant addition to the writings which preceded them. Some of these minor works are preserved in that ill-defined corpus of writings known by the technical name of Pseudepigrapha. The editors of collections known by this name vary slightly in their views as to what properly should be included. The editor of the most scholarly edition, R. H. Charles, groups three works under the heading of 'Ethics and Wisdom Literature'. These are, Fourth Maccabees, Pirke Aboth and the Story of Ahikar. Taking them in the reverse order, we may wish to regard 'Ahikar' as a Wisdom writing. We have previously, in Chapter II, discussed this work in some detail, and there is no need to add anything at this point. The Story of Ahikar is much older than the literature we have been discussing in this chapter, and finds its proper place in the context of Wisdom outside of Israel.

The second work, Pirke Aboth, is fundamentally an ethical work and, in fact, belongs to the Mishna. As its name indicates, it is a collection of 'Sayings of the Fathers', i.e. utterances of Jewish teachers, and covers a period said to extend from the third century B.C. to the third century A.D. It is a collection of maxims, largely ethical and religious. It aimed at gathering into one collection the wisdom of the past rather than at formulating new maxims for the future. It reflects both on

D

piety and Wisdom as these have been handed down by the Fathers. Quite a number of the sayings are similar to those in the Book of Proverbs. One of its great sayings shows to what heights of spiritual insight this collection can rise: 'for the reward of a precept is a precept, and the reward of a sin is a sin' (4:2). Another may be quoted to show the style of writing, which is, of course, one commonly found in Wisdom Literature: 'There are three crowns; the crown of Torah, the crown of priesthood, and the crown of royalty; but the crown of a good name mounts above them' (4:17).

However interesting this tract may be and however valuable its ethical teaching, it does not, in itself, add anything specifically new to what we already know of Wisdom teaching. The truth of the matter is that Pirke Aboth tends, on the whole, to place the emphasis on practical ethics and uses the form of Wisdom writing as a means to teaching its ethics.

The third work we have to consider is Fourth Maccabees. It was composed probably by a Hellenistic Jew of Alexandria, shortly before A.D. 70. It deals, in its own peculiar way, with Wisdom; but the reference is slight and the main interest is in the history of the family of Maccabees considered as martyrs of the Jewish faith. Strictly speaking, it cannot be regarded as Wisdom Literature, but for our purpose it is interesting in what it actually says about Wisdom. One of its aims is to show the superiority of reason, or more accurately, pious reason, over passion. The striking opening sentence of the book gives some idea of the theme it proposes to discuss: 'Philosophical in the highest degree is the question I propose to discuss, namely whether the Inspired Reason is supreme over the passions' (1:1). This sounds rather like Stoic teaching. Yet, when it is examined more closely, it is seen to be quite Jewish. The writer has been influenced both in his vocabulary and subject matter by the Hellenism of his day, say 63 B.C. to A.D. 38. When, however, the author comes to state what he means by Reason, he relates it to Wisdom, and to that Wisdom which belongs to Judaism. Something of the flavour of his way of thinking becomes perceptible at 1:15: 'Reason I take to be the mind preferring with clear deliberation the life of wisdom. Wisdom I take to be the knowledge of things, divine and human, and of their causes.' There is nothing peculiarly Jewish in this, and, indeed, much is to be said for the view that he speaks with the accent of Hellenism. In particular, the phrase 'clear deliberation' is a technical philosophical term. But his very next sentence places him in that line of tradition which traces its ancestry to Moses, and which in his own day had so re-adapted itself that it was prepared to offer a Jewish alternative to the heathen Wisdom of the Greeks. He writes, in continuation of the preceding quotation, 'This I take to be the culture acquired under the Law, through which we learn with due reverence the things of God and for our worldly profit the things of man'. In the wider context of his book, it is necessary to see that even when he uses the Greek word for Law, he is nevertheless thinking in terms of the Law given by God to Moses. Wisdom, as was the case in the Apocrypha, is inseparable from the Jewish Law. This conclusion, of course, brings us back to the position we had reached in the Apocrypha. It would appear, therefore, that if there is to be any further development of the idea of Wisdom, we may have to look beyond the confines of Judaism, and this, in fact, points us towards the New Testament, which will be discussed in a later chapter.

VI.—THREE IMPORTANT ASPECTS OF WISDOM

THE Wisdom writers were able to use the term Wisdom without feeling any need to provide a precise definition. But our previous chapters have shown how varied the term actually is. This is only to be expected when we remember for how many centuries the term had been in use before it entered into the canonical literature, and when we note that the literature continues into the time of the Apocrypha. In order that we may be able to exercise some control over the variety of meanings which may be read into the term wisdom, we propose to discuss it under three rather broad headings. First, Wisdom as a literary category. Secondly, Wisdom as a philosophy of life. Thirdly, Wisdom as an entity. We are not suggesting that these broad divisions are either mutually exclusive, or that they are exact and precise. What may be claimed is that they may help the reader to realize that with the passage of time Wisdom suffered change and development and its end was different from its beginning.

I.—*Wisdom as a Literary Category*

In the earliest stages, Wisdom simply described an utterance or saying. It was a phrase or a sentence coined by people who exercised the gift of memorable expression. These people later on became a recognized class or institution and were designated as 'the wise' or 'sages' or 'wise men'. The sayings they composed expressed in pithy form their reflections on life. At a later stage, these sayings were put into writing and thereby received permanent form, and ultimately were included in the canon of the Old Testament. Indeed, as a literary phenomenon, Wisdom continued beyond the canon and found representation in the Apocrypha. This extended corpus of writings has, in fact, become normative and classical for our understanding of Wisdom today. In all this usage of the term, Wisdom is simply a descriptive term. It designates a distinctive group of writings which emanated from a well-defined group of thinkers and writers. The term Wisdom in this context is parallel to the term 'prophetic' as applied to those other Biblical writings which emanate from the prophets.

However, an examination of the contents of this literature discloses that there are two elements which can be distinguished from one another. First, there is teaching or instruction expressed in the style characteristic of Wisdom Literature; at this level Wisdom is good advice and sober instruction, especially suitable for young men. Secondly, as a presupposition of this teaching or instruction, Wisdom is an attribute, it is the quality or talent which, if possessed, makes a man wise. If you exercise this attribute, then your actions will be characterized by Wisdom. Your utterances will show Wisdom by the kind of advice you give. Your other actions will show Wisdom by the skill with which you execute them, even in a technical matter such as weaving or digging a mine. If you should happen to be a king, then your Wisdom might show itself in your practical ability to make the kind of decisions expected of a king.

Wisdom as including both instruction and attribute, naturally enough, suggests something which can be taught and cultivated. This function, which became somewhat specialized, was largely in the hands of the Wise Men. Under their leadership, the Wisdom Movement strongly developed its didactic side. Wisdom is didactic in the sense that it provides teaching about etiquette, and gives rules and instructions for success in life. But behind the claim of wisdom that it can put a man on the road to success, there lies the assumption that those who practise Wisdom have the right understanding of life and of man's place in the world. Implicit in Wisdom teaching is the presupposition that the world is of such a nature that man can formulate rules and regulations about it. Wisdom has its own beliefs about the kind of world man lives in. It suggests that man can discern an order or system in what to all appearances is the changing flux of life. However, this order is only discernible to the man who applies himself to Wisdom. He who seeks with Wisdom, of course, finds. In this area of activity, Wisdom shows itself as an intellectual instrument or technique for dealing with the world, including human nature itself. Through the application of Wisdom man gains some control over life and attains a greater measure of happiness and prosperity than if he neglected Wisdom. Wisdom is an attribute a man may or may not possess. But it is found, normally, in most men. If he has it, he can become wise, prudent, cool and successful. If he has not got it, he is a fool, rash, hot and a failure. However, it is the aim of the Wisdom teacher, as representing the didactic element in the movement, to cultivate the Wisdom in his pupil and to warn him against the dangers of foolishness. Although the religious element in Wisdom is latent and implicit, it nevertheless presupposes faith in Yahweh. The Wise Men divide men into two groups, those who have wisdom and those who do not. Whether a man has it or not is dependent upon whether or not God has bestowed it upon him. Wisdom has its source in God and, indeed, comes to be regarded as a divine attribute. This view becomes more clearly expressed at a later date, in particular in the Apocrypha, but it may be assumed that it was present, at least implicitly, in the early stages. At any rate, the Wisdom Movement teaches that without Wisdom man loses his way in the world and wanders in the darkness of his foolish mind. Thus we are brought to the point where we have to consider Wisdom as a philosophy of life.

II.—*Wisdom as a Philosophy of Life*

This rather more sophisticated view of Wisdom could only manifest itself when the Wise Men and others were anxiously asking questions about life. This stage could only be reached at a time when men were expressing doubts about the value of this attribute called Wisdom. Men were finding in their own personal experience, and probably also in the experience of the nation, that to possess Wisdom was no guarantee of success or prosperity in this world. Wisdom is being forced to reconsider its own presuppositions. It is being led by circumstance to formulate what the Germans call a *Weltanschauung*, i.e. world-outlook or philosophy of life. Naturally enough, Wisdom as a philosophy of life tends to vary from one writer to another, as, for example, as between the different points of view characteristic of the authors of Job, Ecclesiastes and Ben Sirach. Yet, each one of these in his own way represents an attitude to life and commends it to his contemporaries as a contribution towards dealing with life's problems. What this means may become clearer by paying attention to a feature which is prominent

both in Job and Ecclesiastes. In contrast with the Book
of Proverbs, especially chapters 10 to the end, these
two works are highly critical of current Wisdom teaching.
They attack the norms of orthodox Wisdom. Job, in
particular, rejects the popular theories about man's
destiny and God's role in human affairs. He asserts that
the presuppositions of Wisdom were incapable of handling the problems of the relations between human
righteousness and life's rewards. Wisdom as an attribute
in man did not bring the success the teachers claimed for
it. Wisdom as an attribute in God only increased the
bewilderment of the righteous sufferer. Wisdom as a
body of teaching failed to deal with the problems and
difficulties of life. Job, therefore, is forced to search for
a higher wisdom, of a more comprehensive nature than
anything previously conceived by Wisdom teachers. Job
postulates a hidden wisdom at work in the universe. It is
a secret Wisdom, the nature of which is known only to
God. It was different in its nature from the Wisdom
possessed by man; but it was completely under the
control of God. Indeed, God had decreed that the creation, in all its intricate mystery, was ordered on the
basis of this unique and absolute Wisdom which was His
alone. Because of this Wisdom, so intimately related to
God alone, Job is enabled to leave aside his anguished
concern to solve, personally, the problems which otherwise would have daunted his spirit. The whole creation,
in its stupendous vastness in time and space, is, according to Job, under the control of God, Who is absolute and
supreme in Wisdom.

Here is the raw material for a philosophy of life which
has the divine Wisdom as its basic pre-supposition. The
universe, with its suffering and mystery, expresses the
mind and purpose of the Creator, Who has made all things

and ordered His universe in accordance with His own higher Wisdom. Unfortunately, perhaps, Job's philosophy of life was not developed in any clear way in the literature which came after him. The positive step he had tried to take was not continued. Indeed, the later development by-passed Job, as can be seen in Ecclesiastes. This work is, frequently, negative and offers a pessimistic philosophy of life. The author's incipient cynicism and his gentle scepticism precluded him from making a positive advance in his thinking about the value and functions of Wisdom. He doubts, indeed, if Wisdom is capable of providing an answer to man's questions about life. He agrees, of course, that Wisdom is better than folly, but this is only what we expect from a Wise Man. He indulges too much in negative generalizations, and regards God as remote from human affairs: 'God is in heaven and you upon earth' (5:4). He treats the 'distance' between man and God as if it rendered impossible any personal relationship between them. Wisdom teaching had schooled him to scrutinize the half-truths taught, presumably, by his contemporaries. But at the same time, possibly as a reaction against his critics, he unduly narrowed the scope of Wisdom's operations. He did not envisage the possibility that Wisdom might be a link between God and man, or that there might be a higher, hidden Wisdom of God's at work in the universe. His idea of Wisdom was too tightly pegged down to the human level. He limited it to practical and prosaic rules. His philosophy of life dealt mainly with shrewdness and prudence. It avoids excess. It sounds the admonitory note. Occasionally one may hear in his teaching the still sad music of humanity, but the prevailing note is the negative cry 'vanity of vanities'. Wisdom for him leads on to a pessimistic philosophy of life.

So far as Wisdom in the Apocrypha is concerned, the idea of Wisdom as a philosophy of life tends to recede into the background and a more explicitly religious view of Wisdom is put forward. As indicated in the previous chapter, Wisdom is treated as Jewish rather than universal. Wisdom becomes incorporated, as it were, into the body of Jewish life, national and religious. The task of Wisdom henceforth is not so much to offer a philosophy of life for man *quâ* man in the human situation, as rather to commend Judaism as a faith which has been committed to Israel for the benefit of all who fear the Lord.

III.—*Wisdom as an Entity*

By the use of the word 'entity' as applied to Wisdom, we are drawing attention to the fact that occasionally, and specially in the later literature, Wisdom is regarded as an object, as it were, 'out there' in the world. It is a thing a man may seek to possess or use. It may be an object alongside of God and may stand in an intimate relation to Him. This view of Wisdom goes beyond regarding it as the simple personification of a divine attribute. It is also much more concrete than the view which thinks of wisdom as an attribute to life. That is why we have used the term entity. This term aims simply at emphasizing the fact that Wisdom has an existence of its own, that it operates in many different ways in the relations between God and man.

Several passages illustrate what is meant by referring to Wisdom as an entity. In Job 15:7f there is an allusion to an almost-forgotten myth about primeval man:

'Are you the first man that was born?'

This first man was famous for his Wisdom. It was said that he seized Wisdom from the gods and monopolized it for his own private use. This allusion, directed by Eliphaz to Job, envisages Wisdom as a detached object, existing with some degree of independence from the gods whose property it was, in the first instance. Eliphaz, of course, is only making a mocking allusion, but he says enough to show that he is treating Wisdom as something more than merely a personification of a divine attribute. In Job 28, in its present form, two different conceptions of Wisdom are put side by side in the one chapter. For our purposes the significant verses are 20–27. In that passage, Wisdom is an object of some kind, on its own. It is located in some place, unknown to man and inaccessible in any case. However, God knows all about it, its nature is open to Him and He has utilized it for His own purposes, especially in relation to His act of creation. Both in ch. 15 and ch. 28, Wisdom has been objectified, in the sense that it stands outside, and apart from, God and man. Indeed, some wish to claim that at 28:27f, Wisdom has actually been hypostasized,

> 'then he saw it and declared it;
> he established it, and searched it out.'

That is, Wisdom has been given characteristics and traits of its own, by which it is recognized to be what it is. God, apparently, took account of those characteristic features or qualities which belong to Wisdom. Wisdom here is no bare abstraction, it is an entity. More technically, Wisdom is the bearer or locus of certain characteristics, integrated into a unity, standing over against God as a unity, or man as a unity. It is therefore an entity which is richer and more complex than the personification of the single attribute of Wisdom. But whether it can be called a hypostatis is probably a matter of what that technical term itself really means.

When we turn to Proverbs, especially to the first nine chapters, two interesting facts about Wisdom claim attention. First, the personification of Wisdom is very prominent. It is regarded as a female figure. She is described as a preacher, proclaiming the merits of Wisdom in the public streets. She is referred to as a bride who will never forsake her husband and as a hostess who invites guests to feast at her table. That Wisdom has become personified is not at all surprising. The Old Testament has frequently personified elements in its religious vocabulary, such as the arm of the Lord, righteousness, truth and mercy. What is surprising here is the *kind* of personification. There is almost certainly something additional to normal, literary development at work here. For we have to find an adequate explanation of why Wisdom should become feminine, and to explain why female figures like wife and hostess should find a place in Israel's religious thought. Probably influences of a mythological nature have entered in from the religious mythology of other nations. However, in ch. 8 there are references to Wisdom which go beyond literary personification. In this chapter Wisdom is not only a preacher but makes self-claims about her intrinsic value. She claims a divine origin, prior to the creation. She claims to have been present at the creation, possibly assisting in some way, and most remarkable of all, claims to be a source of delight to God. Obviously the language is highly poetical, but behind it there lies the view of Wisdom as a concrete entity. Wisdom is capable of performing certain functions, such as the power to rule as seen in kings and princes, and he who finds her finds life itself. Doubtless all these and other capabilities of

Wisdom are made possible through God as their ultimate and continuous source. But here again Wisdom is more than a personification, it is a complex entity. It performs certain functions in the relations between God and man. It is an intermediary of some kind having a unique standing with God.

This complex view of Wisdom is found also in the Apocrypha, particularly in the teaching of Ecclesiasticus 24. Wisdom there shows features which liken her to a personal being, capable of self-praise. She exists eternally, is identified with the word of God, and claims to be able to satisfy the spiritual longings of a man's heart. She has some degree of independence from God but is not self-determined in the sense of having a will which might be opposed to God's will. Even Wisdom's dwelling-place in Jerusalem, and her relation to the Law and religion of Israel are determined by God. Wisdom is a unique entity, in the sense of a spiritual object whose sphere of operation is between God and His created order. Similar views about Wisdom as an objective entity are found in the Wisdom of Solomon, in particular chs. 7:22–8:1. Wisdom is a spiritual reality, heavily loaded with some twenty-one virtues bestowed upon her by God. Wisdom is more intimate with God than any other creature and seems to be divine rather than human. Although she has some apparent independence from God she does not act independently of, nor contrary to, God. She is a spiritual being with unique and specialized functions in the divine economy.

Whereas it is clear that Israel reached a point in its thinking where it regarded Wisdom as an objective entity, with peculiar qualities and specialized functions, it is no less clear that the conclusions reached are of a vague and imprecise nature. Israel seemed to go as far as it could go in bringing Wisdom and God together, but it stopped short of making Wisdom a god alongside of God. However, in the later writings, as noted above, Wisdom is placed on what might be called the divine side of the frontier-line between God and man. Yet even to attribute so high a status to Wisdom still leaves a number of unanswered questions about its nature. We shall attempt to say something about this in the next chapter.

VII.—THE FIGURE OF WISDOM

In the preceding chapter we drew attention to the complex nature of the term Wisdom. There we discussed three recognizable aspects of the concept. But, even so, this does not exhaust the meaning of the term. For further consideration of Wisdom suggests that there are occasions when it seems to be regarded as almost, but not quite, a personal being, and as something more than an abstract concept possessing different aspects. There are passages which envisage Wisdom as manifesting characteristics commonly attributed to human beings. Some of those characteristics may simply be due to the use of rather vivid personification. Yet in other passages Wisdom is described as an agent rather than as an agency. For Wisdom, at times, seems to have aims of its own and shows some slight degree of independence from God. At any rate, it is proper that we should consider these passages, in the hope that they will shed further light on the nature of Wisdom.

Within the first nine chapters of Proverbs there are several passages which treat Wisdom more like a personal being than a personified attribute. We refer to 1:20–33; 8:1–35; 9:1–6 (13–18). These speak of Wisdom performing actions normally done by persons. They are deeds of a personal nature, such as preaching, acting as a hostess in one's home, and speaking in praise of oneself. It is difficult to believe that these are the actions solely of an abstract virtue which has been personified. For example, it is unusual to think of a virtue such as Wisdom becoming a hostess inviting guests to her house, and yet say that this is only a literary personification. Obviously something has been added on to the process of personification. If we take the teaching of these three passages together, we see that the personified Wisdom found elsewhere in Proverbs has been supplemented by the addition of several concrete features. Wisdom acts now as a person; she is a woman who exhorts an audience, a hostess who offers hospitality. That the whole concept of Wisdom has become more complex appears evident from the fact that in all these passages Wisdom has become a female figure. We are led to a similar conclusion when we turn to the Apocrypha, and consider Ecclesiasticus 14:20–15:8, 24:1ff, and the Wisdom of Solomon 8:2–16. Ecclesiasticus describes how Wisdom is to be sought and how she will welcome the seeker, and refers to her divine origin. The last passage tells how Solomon desired to have Wisdom as his bride. Both writers use exalted language about Wisdom. She is described variously as woman, wife, mother, bride. She has a house, is of noble birth, beautiful in appearance, to be loved for her many virtues and qualities. The general impression given by these passages is that at this stage in Israel's speculations about Wisdom, she is regarded as something richer and more complex than a literary personification.

It is important also to remember that the above passages in their present form represent a relatively late date in Wisdom Literature. Those from Proverbs may be from the fourth or even third century, and those from Ecclesiasticus and the Wisdom of Solomon in the second century. They will tend, therefore, to represent the culmination of a process of development and will record views about Wisdom which presuppose a previous history of thought about the nature of Wisdom. Indeed, particularly in Proverbs, there is much to suggest that what is said about Wisdom as a female figure may be due to additions made at the latest possible date before the collection was edited in its final form.

In the first nine chapters of Proverbs, taken as a whole, the novel feature is that Wisdom is regarded as a woman. She talks in the first person singular, and speaks in praise of herself. She commands her maidservants to go out and deliver invitations to men that they might come as guests to feast at her table. She provides food and drink which have the power of conferring life. This female Wisdom is also a preacher who stands in public places and exhorts men where they congregate. Indeed, Wisdom is like a prophet, to the extent that she calls upon men to make a decision between Wisdom and folly. Those who accept the invitation of Wisdom receive life (8:35; 9:1–6); those who reject it end in death (9:13–18). Some of the language used by Wisdom herself is so exalted that it would be appropriate in the mouth of God:

'I have counsel and sound wisdom,
I have insight, I have strength.
By me kings reign,
and rulers decree what is just' (8:14f).

Indeed, this is the kind of language applied to God in Isaiah 28, 29 and 31:2.

The important passage Proverbs 8:22–31 makes some special claims on behalf of Wisdom and does so in such a way as to suggest that the Wisdom under discussion is something more complex than the personification of a Divine attribute. Wisdom is created by God and comes into existence prior to the rest of creation. She is said to be present there with God—'I was beside him'—

during the process or act of creation. The language, of course, is highly poetical and a marked degree of ambiguity is attached to some of the terms. Likewise, what functions are supposed to have been fulfilled by Wisdom on this occasion are not stated precisely. A good illustration of the elusive nature of the thought here is provided in verses 30 and 31:

> 'then I was beside him, like a master workman;
> and I was daily his delight,
> rejoicing before him always,
> rejoicing in his inhabited world
> and delighting in the sons of men.'

It is probable that the writer was not in a position to be more precise. His allusive language belonged to the nature of the subject he was discussing. For example, the text does not really say that Wisdom was an agent engaged at work on creation on behalf of God. Further, the words 'like a master workman' are open to suspicion. First, the word 'like' is not in the Hebrew, and secondly, 'master workman' is only one of several equally possible translations. Some have wanted to translate 'master workman' by either 'nursling' or 'guardian'. However, more recent study has tended to avoid a precise or specific name. A more general translation seems to suit the context better, and it has been proposed to translate:

Then was I at his side, a living link (or 'vital bond').[1]

This lack of precise description suggests the view that at this point the idea of Wisdom is in process of being taken beyond the previously established stage of a simple personification of an attribute. The new note sounded in this passage is that of a uniquely close relationship be-

[1] R. B. Y. Scott, *Vetus Testamentum*, Vol. X, p. 222, April 1960.

tween Wisdom and God. Wisdom is closer to God than
man is. She is His associate, but in a manner that can
only be hinted at and not defined. She is there, beside
God, in a way no other creature could be. She commends
Wisdom to mankind by the sheer attractiveness of her
nature, and her charms form a strong contrast to the
impersonal manner of traditional Wisdom teachers. The
noteworthy feature in this enriched conception of Wisdom
has been expressed thus, 'wisdom does not turn towards
man in the shape of an "It", teaching guidance, salvation
or the like, but of a person, a summoning "I".[1]

Support for this view of the change towards a more
personal conception of Wisdom comes from Ecclesiasticus and from the Wisdom of Solomon. In the former,
14:20–15:8, Wisdom is a female figure. She is described
as a mother and a wife. She calls men to a feast and acts
as hostess. In the Wisdom of Solomon, 8:2f the bridal
metaphor is used and her beauty praised:

'I loved her and sought her from my youth,
  and I desired to take her for my bride.'

Both Ecclesiasticus and the Wisdom of Solomon (ch. 24)
use rather exalted language concerning Wisdom. She is
eternal, comes down from heaven to earth, sits by God's
throne, and ministers in the temple at Jerusalem.

Whatever led to so many feminine features being bestowed upon the figure of Wisdom, the explanation
seems to demand something more concrete than a
gradual literary evolution from a personification of an
abstract virtue like Wisdom. We have to remember that
the Old Testament resolutely excluded feminine elements
from its thought about God. The general trend of
theological reflection in Israel would form a barrier

[1] *Old Testament Theology*, Vol. I, p. 444, Gerhard von Rad.

against bringing a female into the idea of deity. Doubtless, despite that trend, it was only natural that when
Wisdom did, as a matter of fact, become personified, the
term took a feminine form. This would be facilitated by
the fact that the word for Wisdom in Hebrew is of
feminine gender. But what actually were the factors at
work which led to the emphasis upon the feminine side
of Wisdom? Several answers have been offered, of which
the most probable are the following.

It has been suggested that Wisdom as a female figure
in Israel has arisen from the influence of myths which
were current outside Israel. It is true, of course, that
there are mythological figures which are said to possess
Wisdom as one of their many attributes. But there seems
to be no evidence to prove there was a goddess known by
the name of Wisdom who might have served as a prototype for the figure of Wisdom. Nevertheless, it has been
claimed that there was a Canaanite goddess with the
name of Hokmoth. According to this theory, Hokmoth
is said to be a Phoenician form of the word Wisdom.
This, in turn, is related to the Hebrew word for Wisdom,
hokmah. Interestingly enough, the form Hokmoth is also
found a few times in Hebrew Wisdom literature. The
inter-relation of those terms, applied to a goddess and to
Wisdom, is taken to provide a clue for the claim that
there was a mother-goddess, with a fertility cult, connected with Wisdom. The inference is, of course, that
Judaism has been influenced by this tradition in the
formation of its own peculiar conception of Wisdom.
But not all who have examined this view are convinced
by it. Too much weight has been placed on the occurrence of the term *hokmoth* in Hebrew. This may really be
no more than a synonym for *hokmah*, and simply a later
form of the word. If this is so, and it appears probable,

then it casts doubt on the claim that Hebrew Wisdom is based on a goddess called Hokmoth, and that the feminine features in Hebrew Wisdom have been derived from such a goddess.

Another view of the figure of Wisdom is one which connects it with an aretalogy, in which the goddess Isis is praised for her many virtues. The aretalogy is composed of some fifty-seven ascriptions of praise to Isis. The first may be translated thus:

'I am Isis, the ruler of every land . . .'

Other utterances in self-praise are:

'I appointed laws for men—.'
'I am the oldest daughter of Kronos.'
'I am the wife and sister of King Oseiridos.'
'I separated earth and heaven.'

The literary convention of using the 'I' of the first person singular recalls Proverbs 8, especially verses 22–30, and also Ecclesiasticus 24. It is claimed, on the basis of this aretalogy, that 'the figure of Wisdom in Ecclesiasticus shows a startling affinity to a Syrian Astarte with the features of Isis'.[1] The inference drawn by Knox is that Judaism was in danger because of a revised Isis-Sarapis cult which was established by Ptolemy about 300 B.C. He adds, 'it is not unnatural that Jewish monotheism . . . might be seriously threatened by a semi-official cultus of this type, which was compatible with a high morality, and could be interpreted in a more or less monotheistic sense . . . young Jews seeking advancement under the Ptolemaic dynasty might find it hard to

[1] W. L. Knox, *Journal of Theological Studies*, Vol. XXXVIII, July 1937, p. 235.

resist the attractions of Isis'. Knox believes that it was because of this danger to its faith that Judaism found a sanction for the personification of Wisdom as a female figure. He writes: 'The personified Wisdom is the answer of orthodox Judaism: the source of order in creation and conduct is not Isis, but the Wisdom of God. Wisdom had already been canonized as the nature of God and the ideal of man; she now becomes personified.'[1]

It may be that some of the credit ascribed to 'orthodox Judaism' in the above quotation should be transferred to the account of Wisdom thinkers within Judaism. But Knox's conclusion can be accepted as it stands: 'The figure of Wisdom has been modified to meet a change in the nature of the danger'.[2] The feminine features in Wisdom were a necessary element in the appeal that Judaism was making both to the faithful Jew and to the Gentile who evinced an interest in Judaism.

There is a third view concerning the origin of Wisdom which traces it to a Persian source; but the claim here is of a more general kind, not specifically related to Wisdom as a female figure. Persian religion included the existence of some six intermediaries which functioned between the supreme God and the world. Several of these intermediaries have been thought to have provided a model for Hebrew Wisdom. One of these is *Armaiti*, which was known as Wisdom among some Greek writers. Another is *Vohu mano* which was said to bear a resemblance to Logos as used by Philo. But as Rankin says, 'It is unlikely that any particular one of the Persian intermediaries contributed all to the Jewish conception of Wisdom'.[3] He himself thinks the figure of Asha 'provides a much closer analogy to Wisdom than does either *Vohu*

---

[1] *Ib.* 236.   [2] *Ib.* 237.
[3] *Israel's Wisdom Literature*, p. 246, O. S. Rankin.

mano or *Armaiti*.[1] However, the relationship between Persian religion and Judaism at this point seems too general to be considered as offering a prototype for the female figure in Hebrew Wisdom.

The brief references to those three views about outside influences at work on the kind of figure Hebrew Wisdom came to be, serve to show that Judaism was forced to take measures in order to safeguard the purity of its own faith in God. Traditionally Israel had always reacted negatively against any suggestion that a female figure should be brought into its thinking about God. History itself supplies some illustrations of this point of view. In 1 Kings 15:13, King Asa is praised for removing and burning 'an abominable image made for Asherah', where Asherah appears to represent Astarte. Another illustration comes from outside what might be called 'normative Judaism'. It concerns the famous Jewish military colony at Elephantiné on the Nile. The religion there, which flourished in the fifth century B.C., deviated from Palestinian Judaism to the extent that other gods were worshipped alongside Yahweh. One of them was a female god, named Anath-Yahu. This strange deviation among people who considered themselves to be Jewish may illustrate how easy it was for the feminine element to enter into the idea of the godhead, once there is a relaxation of strict monotheism.

When we come, say, to the fourth century B.C. and later, to include some parts of Proverbs 1–9, Ecclesiasticus and the Wisdom of Solomon, we notice, of course, a readiness to accept the presence of a female figure, Wisdom, with Judaism. At this stage Wisdom is given a very high place in Jewish religious thought, but not the supreme one. Yahweh is unchallengeably supreme.

[1] *Ib.* 250.

Wisdom is accepted, and indeed commended, to younger Jews and to serious elders, including Gentiles, as the Jewish counterpart to the attractions of the goddess of love or fertility, whether known as Astarte or Asherah or Isis or even as the Queen of Heaven. But Wisdom is never equated with Yahweh nor identified with Him. She is not His paramour nor His wife. Basically, Wisdom is still a personification, and not strictly speaking a hypostasis. Specific feminine features have been added to this basic personification, such as bride, wife, hostess, etc. These may well have appealed to the emotional side of human nature, but it is important to notice that these features have been treated with dignity and restraint; they have been raised to the highest moral level and made acceptable to the guardians of orthodox Judaism.

Some degree of support for this view may be derived from Prov 9:13–18. The subject discussed there is female folly in deliberate contrast with female wisdom. Jews are warned against her. Her shamelessness, promiscuity and immorality are exposed. She seeks to batten on the immature and the less intelligent. Acceptance of her way of life ends in death. In contrast with what is said about Wisdom, this Madam Folly is thus described:

'A foolish woman is noisy;
she is wanton and knows no shame.'

The fate of those who accept her invitation is described:

'But he does not know that the dead are there,
that her guests are in the depths of Sheol.'

It is in answer to that kind of danger that the contribution of the Wisdom thinkers to Judaism is to be discerned. In a period of crisis, when traditional Judaism was losing its hold, Wisdom thinkers propounded a new and richer concept of Wisdom, with the aim of rendering Judaism attractive to the thinkers of their own day. The figure of Wisdom became Judaism's way of explaining the relations between God and man, and between God and the world He had created. By this way of thinking Wisdom is put forward as a spiritual reality. Wisdom is the connecting link between the Creator and all that is created. Wisdom has her source in God. It, or she, was His first creation. She has, as it were, an ancient pedigree which can be traced back to before the creation. Although she is a creature, nevertheless, now that she has been created, she is eternal. Wisdom represents God's presence in the world. She is the way or the mode in which God operates in the world. The creation itself manifests the Wisdom of God. This is a significant development in the Jewish idea of God. The traditional emphasis on the Divine Transcendence, traceable back to the time of Moses, is now balanced by an awareness of the Divine Immanence. God is seen to be immanent in the Creation through the presence in it of the Divine Wisdom.

VIII.—WISDOM AND THE NEW TESTAMENT

STRICTLY speaking, Wisdom Literature as a literary
category is not found in the New Testament; but the
figure of Wisdom, and Wisdom as a way of thinking
about life, exert quite an influence within the New
Testament itself. As the preceding chapters have shown,
Wisdom had become integrated with Jewish ways of
thinking about God and the world He had created.
Through recourse to the figure of Wisdom, the pious Jew
was able to give a satisfactory explanation of how the
world came into existence, and, perhaps more important,
of how a man could obtain those qualities which would
enable him to live a successful life. Because the New
Testament has so many roots embedded in the soil of
Judaism, it is inevitable that hints and traces of Wisdom
should be found in its pages. In fact, Wisdom is much
more pervasive in the New Testament than is commonly
thought. Naturally enough, so skilful a teacher as our
Lord does not hesitate to quote a popular proverb, such
as might have been produced by a Wisdom writer in a
past age, in order to emphasize some fairly obvious truth.
A good example is, 'Wherever the body is, there the
eagles will be gathered together' (Matt 24:17, Luke
17:37). But there are other utterances of our Lord, and
other passages in the New Testament, which are more
intimately connected with the Wisdom Movement than
any mere quotation of a proverb might indicate. If we
look first at the closing words of the Sermon on the Mount

(Matt 7:24–27), we shall see a style of utterance which closely resembles the way in which Wisdom teachers addressed a challenge to their audiences. It will be recalled that these closing verses describe the contrast in behaviour between two builders. One built on a good foundation, and the other on sand. The former is wise, the latter foolish. 'Every one, then, who hears these words of mine and does them will be like a wise man . . . and every one who hears these words of mine and does not do them will be like a foolish man.'

Here we see Jesus appealing to the traditional division, accepted by Wisdom teachers, of two categories among men. Jesus continues the technique of teaching already established by the Wisdom Movement and used it as a naturally suitable method for presenting His own teaching.

If we examine some other passages in the gospels, we shall soon see that there are several which recall the poetic form of the Book of Proverbs. The following examples may be regarded as typical. We have ventured to present them in a form which draws attention to their poetic rather than their prose style:

(a) 'Ask, and it will be given you;
    Seek, and you will find;
    Knock, and it will be opened to you' (Matt 7:7).

(b) 'Every one who exalts himself will be humbled,
    and he who humbles himself will be exalted'
                    (Luke 14:11, 18:14; Matt 23:12).

(c) 'If your hand causes you to sin, cut it off;
    It is better for you to enter life maimed
    than with two hands to go to hell' (Mark 9:43).

Outside the gospels, and still limiting ourselves to literary rather than theological affinities, the Epistle of

James shows many resemblances to Wisdom Literature. It contains many moral maxims and pithy sayings, and several of these deal with the subject of Wisdom. James tends to avoid speculation but shows a deep concern for moral conduct. So far as Wisdom is concerned, he seems to be dealing with certain opponents who were interested in the claims of a heavenly Wisdom which was said to have come down from heaven to earth. According to James, the test of the genuineness of this alleged Wisdom must be an ethical one. True Wisdom is known by its fruits. James writes,

'But if you have bitter jealousy and selfish ambition in your hearts, do not boast and be false to the truth. This wisdom is not such as comes down from above, but is earthly, unspiritual, devilish' (3:14).

In contrast with this alleged Wisdom, the fruits of true Wisdom are described in the following terms:

'But the wisdom from above is first pure, then peaceable, gentle, open to reason, full of mercy and good fruits, without uncertainty or insincerity' (3:17).

It is clear that James thinks of Wisdom in practical and ethical terms. He teaches that Wisdom is a gift from God, bestowed on man as a result of prayer. Wisdom, clearly, has been taken right into the centre of the religious life:

'If any of you lacks wisdom, let him ask God, . . . and it will be given him' (1:5).

Further, Wisdom is the power which enables a man to steer his way through the stormy seas of life; therefore the important thing is to be able to distinguish between true and false Wisdom:

'By his good life let him show his works in the meekness of wisdom' (3:13).

James shows some points of resemblance to teaching found in Ecclesiasticus and in the Wisdom of Solomon. He writes (1:9) 'Let the lowly brother boast in his exaltation', whereas Ecclesiasticus (1:11) writes 'The wisdom of a humble man will lift up his head'. It will be recalled that the Wisdom of Solomon, 7:22f, ascribes some twenty-one qualities to Wisdom. James uses a lesser number, perhaps nine, and describes Wisdom as 'first pure, then peaceable, gentle, open to reason, full of mercy and good fruits, without uncertainty or insincerity'.

James continues the tradition of the wise man as one who is prudent and humble. The possession of Wisdom results in carefulness of speech, avoidance of worldliness (4:4). To be truly wise, one must 'be quick to hear, slow to speak, slow to anger' (1:19).

Additional literary allusions to Wisdom are found in The Revelation to John. These are rather different in style and tone from those in James, but possess an interest of their own. They relate themselves more closely to John's understanding of the person of Jesus Christ. Two of these occur in doxologies:

> 'Worthy is the Lamb who was slain, to receive power and wealth and wisdom and might and honour and glory and blessing!' (5:12).

In this first example, Wisdom is but one of seven different attributes. The second example is 7:12, and it, too, regards Wisdom as one of seven attributes. It is probable that the number seven is meant to convey the idea of completeness.

Elsewhere in Revelation Wisdom appears to be a human attribute. This is seen in what can be described as the vision of the Second Beast, at 13:18. The vision is followed by a comment: 'This calls for wisdom'. Apparently Christians need this Wisdom in order to understand the meaning of the vision. A further reference to the need of Wisdom occurs in chapter 17. In that chapter, one of the seven angels refers to 'the mystery of the woman' (v. 7), and in v. 9 says, 'This calls for a mind with wisdom'. In these two instances, Wisdom represents that power evinced, in an eminent degree, by two men in the Old Testament noted for their Wisdom. These are Joseph, on the occasion when he interpreted Pharaoh's dream (Gen 41:39), and Daniel (5:14), where Belshazzer refers to Daniel's 'excellent wisdom', even before Daniel had interpreted his dream. The book of Revelation, of course, not only recalls this old tradition of Wisdom, as manifesting itself in the power to interpret dreams, but adds the reminder that, in the Christian dispensation, Wisdom is one of the attributes of the Lamb of God.

Our discussion of Wisdom in the New Testament, so far, has limited itself, in the main, to the form or literary style; it has been chiefly a discussion of the meaning of the term Wisdom itself, or a reference to the manner in which the teaching is presented. However, if we now turn to the Gospels of Matthew and Luke and examine some passages rather more closely, we shall see how Wisdom exerted an influence on the kind of teaching given by Our Lord Himself. In a later chapter we hope to discuss how Wisdom enabled the first Christians to come to a deeper understanding of the person of Jesus Christ. We propose, therefore, in the remainder of this chapter, to discuss in some detail aspects of the influence of Wisdom in the writings of Matthew and Luke.

A number of passages in these two gospels are parallel to one another. Thus we shall be able to discuss them in pairs. Naturally, we shall have to take each pair, as it were, one pair at a time. But what we shall be attempting to understand is their cumulative effect, and we shall seek to bring together, into a unity, the conclusions to be derived from them as a whole.

(*a*) Matt 11:16–19; Luke 7:31–35

Children at Play

Jesus is depicted as directing criticism against those of his contemporaries who had rejected Him and John the Baptist for very different reasons. They rejected the Baptist because he was austere, 'neither eating nor drinking', whereas they rejected Jesus because He was, so they said, 'a glutton and a drunkard'. Matthew ends his version with the words, 'Yet wisdom is justified by her deeds'. Luke has a slightly different ending, 'Yet wisdom is justified by all her children'. Luke's rendering seems to be the more acceptable, but for our purposes attention has to be directed to 'wisdom' in this context. Wisdom, here, is personified. But even so, there is a variety of opinions as to the meaning of Wisdom in the saying attributed to Jesus. Some have thought of it as referring to Wisdom as generally found in the Old Testament. Others have suggested that 'wisdom' here is the title of an apocryphal book, now lost, and the saying is presumably a quotation from that book. Again it has been thought that Jesus is expressing a decree of the divine Wisdom, or even that He was referring to some of His own teaching, given on an earlier occasion. The most probable explanation seems to be that Jesus is claiming that both his own teaching and that of the Baptist will be vindicated by later events, even although so many of their contemporaries reject it. In any case, whatever explanation is to be preferred, Wisdom is used here in a personified sense.

(b) Matt 11:25–30; Luke 10:21

Truths hidden from the Wise

In the verse preserved in common by Matthew and Luke, there is agreement about the wording, 'I thank thee, Father, Lord of Heaven and Earth, that Thou hast hidden these things from the wise and understanding and revealed them to babes'.

The idea here is that the method by which the divine Wisdom works is understood by the unsophisticated, who really possess true Wisdom, whereas the sophisticated fail to apprehend it. This view is closely connected with the teaching of Paul who contrasts those who pride themselves on possessing 'a wisdom of this age' with those whom Paul calls 'the mature' (1 Cor 2:6). Matthew's longer version provides a background for the saying attributed to Jesus, and some of the terms used recall a few of the phrases used about Wisdom in the book of Sirach. In Matthew 11:28–30 in particular, the use of words like 'yoke', 'rest', 'heavy-laden' should be noted; also, in these verses, Jesus speaks in the first person singular, and speaks in self-recommendation of the benefits He can confer on those who turn to Him. These words and the self-recommendation recall the language and behaviour of Wisdom in Sirach. Attention should be paid to the following where the subject is Wisdom:

'For at last you will find the rest she gives . . .' (6:28).

'Her yoke is a golden ornament . . .' (6:30).

'Come to me, you who desire me' (24:19).

'Draw near to me, you who are untaught . . .' (51:23).

'Put your neck under the yoke,
and let your souls receive instruction . . .' (51:26).

'See with your eyes that I have laboured little and
found for myself much rest' (51:27).

In addition to the employment of the vocabulary of
Wisdom teaching, there is, too, the self-recommendation
used by Jesus which is found also in Sirach, and indeed
goes back to Wisdom in the Book of Proverbs. In addition to Sirach 24:19 and 51:23 quoted above, perhaps a
few other verses from Sirach may be quoted:

'For the remembrance of me is sweeter than honey,
and my inheritance sweeter than the honeycomb.
Those who eat me will hunger for more, and those who
drink me will thirst for more. Whoever obeys me will
not be put to shame, and those who work with my
help will not sin' (24:20–22).

'I opened my mouth and said,
Get these things for yourselves without money' (51:25).

The last line reads 'It is to be found close by' (51:26).

Here Wisdom is saying that the yoke of Wisdom, and
instruction concerning Wisdom, is to be obtained from
her, i.e. the speaker who is recommending herself to the
listeners.

It is perhaps wise to remember that however un-
acceptable it may be to our modern, civilized tastes to
use speech which draws attention to the merits and
qualities of the speaker, no such inhibition hindered self-
recommendation among those who belonged to the
Semitic world, even up to the time of Jesus. Such a
tradition is well vouched for in the Old Testament, and
in relation to the self-recommendation of Wisdom,
Proverbs 1:20–33 is a good illustration. We quote only
v. 23, where Wisdom is the speaker:

E

'Give heed to my reproof;
Behold, I will pour out my thoughts to you;
I will make my words known to you.'

When, therefore, our Lord emphatically draws attention
to Himself with the use of 'I' and 'me' at Matt 11:25–30,
we are not to imagine He was thrusting Himself forward
in a self-centred, egotistical way. Rather it is the reverse.
He is simply accepting the normal way, established by
centuries of practice, by which a Wisdom-teacher commended his instruction to those who had ears to hear.
From what has just been said, it is clear that Jesus made
ready use of the tradition of teaching, both in vocabulary
and in style of presentation, which had been established
by Wisdom teachers down through the centuries.

(c) Matt 12:42; Luke 11:31

Wisdom and the Queen of the South

The form given in Matthew will serve our purposes,
and in any case, the phrase we propose to discuss is
common to both Matthew and Luke:

'The Queen of the South will arise at the judgment
with this generation and condemn it; for she came
from the ends of the earth to hear the wisdom of
Solomon, and, behold, something greater than Solomon
is here.'

This verse may contain an allusion to Matt 11:25–30,
in the sense that it claims that those who turn to Jesus
for Wisdom will receive more than even the Queen of
Sheba received from Solomon (1 Kings 10:1–10). The
significant words are, 'behold, something greater than
Solomon is here'. This claim of Jesus is true despite the
fact that He was rejected by His own generation. Doubt-

less, too, Solomon was regarded as a very wise king. But in Jesus, more than a wise man or even the wisest of men is present; in Jesus, Wisdom in its very self is present.

It is probably significant that this claim is put in the mouth of Jesus Himself. If, as may well be the case, Matt 12:42 and Luke 11:31 go back to an Aramaic[1] original, then these verses may be an example, suggesting that Jesus could use the category of Wisdom as a means of expressing His thoughts about Himself.

(d) Matt 23:34–36; Luke 11:49–51

The Sending of Wise Men

The passage is too long to be quoted in its entirety, but an important difference between the two versions requires to be noted:

'Therefore I send you prophets and wise men . . .' (Matt 23:34).

'Therefore also the Wisdom of God said, "I will send them prophets and apostles . . ."' (Luke 11:49).

In the passages as a whole, Jesus utters a threat against His contemporaries in Jerusalem. The differences between the two passages, so far as the speaker of the threat is concerned, are worthy of note. First, Matthew speaks of 'wise men', whereas Luke refers to 'apostles'. Here we have what may be little more than a difference of emphasis between two traditions, the one emphasizing the Jewish background, the other the Christian one. The second difference, however, is more involved. Matthew preserves the tradition which makes Jesus say that it was He personally who commissioned prophets, wise

[1] cf. M. Black, *An Aramaic Approach to the Gospels and Acts*, pp. 41, 68, 97.

men and scribes. Luke, of course, ascribes the sending, not explicitly to Jesus but to 'the Wisdom of God'.

Closer examination of the two passages shows other slight but interesting differences. For example, Matthew draws attention to the separation between Jesus and the scribes and Pharisees. He refers to them in terms of 'you' and 'yours'. But Luke is a little less direct and speaks of them as 'they' and 'them'. These differences may well go back to the differences in the original sources preserved by Matthew and Luke. However, the more important question before us is to see the relationship between the 'I' used in Matthew, and the 'Wisdom of God' used in Luke. (Perhaps at this point we should insert a warning against too quickly reading into these passages the Christology of Paul, in which he refers to Christ as 'the Wisdom of God' (1 Cor 1:24), especially in view of the fact that we shall discuss Paul's teaching on Wisdom in a later chapter.) To return to Matt 23:34, it is difficult to believe that, in a sense that could be understood by his original hearers, Jesus would have claimed that He personally had sent prophets, wise men and scribes. Further, the phrase in Luke, 'the Wisdom of God', is capable of rather different interpretations. It has been thought to refer to a quotation from an apocryphal writing. Some have seen it as a reference to Paul's teaching about Christ as the Wisdom of God. Others trace the idea to the Old Testament, specifically to 2 Chron 24:19f, which says that God 'sent prophets among them'. The most probable meaning is that it is a periphrasis with a meaning rather like 'God in His wisdom said, I will send . . .'.

Despite the limitations attaching to the presence of Wisdom ideas in these passages, two quite important points emerge. First, the language used of Wisdom in

Luke envisages what might be called a 'quasi-personified wisdom', which is thought of as commissioning wise men. Second, although Matthew does not use Wisdom language, yet in this passage as a whole, and in its continuation in the verses immediately following (vv. 37–39), he ascribes to Jesus functions which are traditionally associated with Wisdom. A comparison between Matt 23:34–39 and Proverbs 1:24–30 shows the close connection between the rejection of Wisdom in the one case and the rejection of Jesus in the other, and the inevitable punishment which follows the rejection. The significance of the relation between Jesus and Wisdom becomes clearer when we consider the next pair of passages.

(e) Matt 23:37–39; Luke 13:34

Lament over Jerusalem

The Matthean passage is a natural and unbroken continuation of Matt 23:34–36, but this Lukan passage, 13:34, is broken off from Luke 11:49–51 and placed in a different context. Neither of the two passages uses Wisdom phraseology. Further, both passages are clearly eschatological and place emphasis upon the impending punishment as a consequence of rejecting Jesus. Nevertheless, the thought contained in the passages and the aims expressed in them are characterized by Wisdom teaching. First, as indicated in the preceding section, the threat of doom because of the rejection of Jesus recalls the threat uttered by Wisdom recorded in Proverbs 1:24–30:

'Because I have called and you refused to listen,
and you have ignored all my counsel,
I also will laugh at your calamity;
I will mock when panic strikes you,

> when panic strikes you like a storm,
> and your calamity comes like a whirlwind,
> when distress and anguish come upon you.'

This kind of language is not far from that of Jesus, 'Behold, your house is forsaken and desolate' (Matt 23:38; Luke 13:35).

Further, the appeal made by Jesus to Jerusalem contains undertones of the kind of language used in Sirach about the connection between Wisdom and Jerusalem. The relevant passage is Sirach 24:7–12, from which verses 8, 10 and 11 may be quoted, Wisdom being the speaker:

> 'Then the Creator of all things gave me a commandment, and the one who created me assigned a place for my tent,
> And he said, "Make your dwelling in Jacob, and in Israel receive your inheritance",
> In the holy tabernacle I ministered before him,
> and so I was established in Zion.
> In the beloved city likewise he gave me a resting place,
> and in Jerusalem was my dominion.'

In Matthew and Luke, the claim implicit in the words of Jesus is that his presence in, and acceptance by, Jerusalem would have safeguarded the well-being of its inhabitants:

> 'O Jerusalem, Jerusalem, killing the prophets and stoning those who are sent to you! How often would I have gathered your children together, as a hen gathers her brood under her wings, and you would not!' (Matt 23:37; Luke 13:34).

Jesus seems to claim for Himself a significance in relation to Jerusalem which recalls the intimate relation between

Wisdom and Jerusalem as recorded in the Wisdom teaching of Sirach.

The survey we have just completed draws attention to the pervasive presence of Wisdom in the New Testament, and in particular to the close relation between Jesus and Wisdom. It may be helpful to draw together some of the conclusions which seem to be important.

There are three simple points which require to be borne in mind. First, Jesus seems to take up quite spontaneously the Wisdom method of teaching, as it had been perfected and refined over the centuries within Israel. There is a naturalness and shrewdness in His pithy observations about human behaviour. In His approach to His audiences He offers a marked contrast to the scholastic style of the scribes and pharisees. His affinities are much nearer to the popular style of the Wisdom teachers of the Old Testament. The Wisdom teachers had shaped a tool by which a speaker could gain entry into the mind of the ordinary man. Jesus took this tool into His own hands, and used it, not just to commend traditional Wisdom, but to preach the Gospel. Secondly, Jesus is very free even in the degree of attachment He had to Wisdom teachers. He is much more than a follower of their methods. Even in His treatment of Wisdom, whether regarded as a figure or as some kind of theological concept, He differs from the teachers in the past. He does not appear to be discussing at any stage a vague, elusive figure called Wisdom. He has no discernible interest in the relations, if any, between Wisdom and Creation, or a hypostatized Wisdom and God. His interests are practical rather than speculative. He is prepared to use Wisdom teaching and vocabulary, but instead of commending Wisdom itself, He makes claims for Himself. He offers Himself to men as the one sure source of all the blessings previously linked with the figure of Wisdom. It is He Who will give men rest and peace: He will satisfy the needs of the heavy-laden; He appeals to the simple and unsophisticated. Behind his allusions to Wisdom there is the implicit hint that Wisdom reaches its fulfilment in Him. All that men looked for and hoped for in Wisdom is to be found, not in an hypostatized attribute of God, but in Him. Thirdly, Jesus does not propound a Wisdom theology or Christology; such teaching could only come later. But in the light of what He says about Wisdom in relation to the response of people to His ministry it is clear that He projected ideas which connected Him and Wisdom in an intimate way. He raises questions about the place of Wisdom as a factor in God's way of life for man. But, as we have said, this is expressed allusively. His attitude to Wisdom might be likened to a photographic negative in process of development. The picture is there but it is not clear, and requires to be brought into focus. Or, to change the simile, further reflection on the significance of Jesus Himself was needed, in order to appreciate better the relations between Him and Wisdom. This task was left to Paul, and in the next chapter we propose to discuss his treatment of the subject.

IX.—PAUL AND WISDOM

As might be expected, Paul uses the term Wisdom in different ways. First, he uses it simply as an attribute to be found both in God and man. Secondly, he thinks of a divine Wisdom, possessed by God alone. The contents of this divine Wisdom constituted a mystery; God, however, was pleased to reveal this mystery to Christians, and this, in turn, was a manifestation of His Wisdom. The third use is peculiar, in that Paul applies Wisdom as an epithet to Jesus Christ. This last use is connected with the fact that Paul relates the figure of Wisdom to his understanding of the person of Jesus Christ. This, of course, approaches what is called a Wisdom Christology. It is a rather complicated and technical subject and we shall treat it only incidentally in this chapter. Our present aim will be limited to an attempt to articulate Paul's different uses of the term Wisdom, and the thought processes which led him to apply it to Jesus Christ. A fuller discussion of Christology will be considered in the next chapter.

A point of entry into Paul's thinking on Wisdom is provided by the three opening chapters of First Corinthians. These chapters indicate the presuppositions of Paul's thoughts on the subject. He starts off with the general distinction between divine and human Wisdom. In 1 Cor 1:17, he draws attention to the difference between 'eloquent wisdom' and 'the cross of Christ'. At first sight the two phrases seem incommensurable; but light is thrown on the working of Paul's mind when we

E*

see him, as it were, interrupting the flow of his own words, by a quotation from the Old Testament:

'I will destroy the wisdom of the wise,
and the cleverness of the clever I will thwart'.

These words are based on Isaiah 29:14. Paul has referred to the historical situation depicted by the prophet. It deals with the frustration experienced by the politicians in Israel as a result of their failure to handle wisely the threat of the Assyrian invasion. Paul uses this incident as an illustration to show the contrast between the divine Wisdom and the cleverness of the worldly-wise leaders. He condemns their cleverness and describes it as 'the wisdom of the world' (v. 20). Such cleverness, however, is foolishness in the sight of God. It was foolish, largely because it was incapable of leading to knowledge of God. Paul then turns to the situation in his own day and says that sophisticated people, like some of the prominent figures in Corinth, were still seeking after the wrong kind of Wisdom. The Wisdom they sought would, no less inevitably, end in failure, because it was incapable of leading men to God.

As already indicated, Paul takes as a basic pre-supposition the infinite difference between human and divine Wisdom. This is something qualitative rather than quantitative. It is as if they operated on two different levels. Some confirmation of this view can be derived from a glance at the two doxologies used by Paul in his Epistle to the Romans. The first and longer one is 11:33-36 and the second, 16:27. The latter is brief, 'the only wise God', and for our purposes may be subsumed under what we propose to say about 11:33-36. It will be observed that the doxology as a whole moves on an exalted level:

'O the depths of the riches and wisdom and knowledge of God' (v. 33).

It celebrates the inscrutable depths in God. It deals only and solely with the divine Wisdom. This is so glorious that no human mind can comprehend its depths. It belongs to that God whom no one can advise and who is under no obligation to anyone outside Himself. This Wisdom belongs to His sublime self-sufficiency. Paul expresses this claim about the divine Wisdom in a series of rhetorical questions, which, naturally enough, expect a negative answer:

'For who has known the mind of the Lord, or who has been his counsellor?' (v. 34).

By means of this kind of language Paul is declaring his agreement with that view of the divine Wisdom which had been taught by the Wisdom teachers in the past and was accepted by Judaism as a whole, even in his own day. Such teaching was the end-product of a long line of development through the centuries, within the Wisdom tradition in Israel. It is the affirmation of the belief that there is a transcendent Wisdom. By its very nature it excludes any possible assimilation to human Wisdom as exercised by man. But, it may be asked, what was the place of Wisdom in Paul's own personal thinking? How is it that Paul, the Christian, can bring together in his thought the fact of Jesus Christ and the current Jewish speculation on Wisdom?

An answer to this question may be gained by returning to those three chapters of First Corinthians with which we began. Two features in Paul's teaching in that passage call for extended comment. The first is Paul's reference to a secret Wisdom, and the second his use of Wisdom as a descriptive category applied to Jesus Christ. Paul

claims there is a secret Wisdom, known to God but revealed by Him to mature Christians only. In 2:6, 7
'. . . it is not a wisdom of this age or of the rulers of this
age', but it is 'a secret and hidden wisdom of God, which
God decreed before the ages'. Although Paul is using the
term Wisdom in a popular manner, nevertheless he is
adding to it a new emphasis. He is making a discrimination within the term itself. He is distinguishing between
Wisdom as manifested by the worldly-wise, and that
Wisdom which is found only among mature Christians.
The former represent the 'wisdom of this age', the latter
represent the Wisdom of the spiritually mature. This
latter Wisdom might conceivably be called Christian
Wisdom or the New Age Wisdom. But it is not a human
achievement nor a natural talent. On the contrary, it is
a gift of God, imparted to man by God the Spirit. In a
sense, it is incomprehensible to the worldly-wise. Further,
not all Christians are in full possession of it. It is not
possessed by 'babes in Christ' (3:1), but only by the
spiritually mature. It might be claimed here that Paul
is teaching the Corinthians a new truth about Wisdom.
He is asserting that unspiritual people cannot comprehend
the Wisdom which is characteristic of, and indeed exclusive to, the Gospel. The conditions of Wisdom are
not simply intellectual but spiritual. Only those who
respond in spirit can receive the Wisdom the Gospel
offers:

'What no eye has seen, nor ear heard, nor the heart of
man conceived,
what God has prepared for those who love him' (2:9).

The reception of such a gift is possible only to those
who are prepared to be regarded as fools by the worldly-
wise:

'Let no one deceive himself. If any one among you thinks he is wise in this age, let him become a fool that he may become wise' (3:18).

It is by means of this Wisdom that the mature Christian apprehends the mystery of God's plan for the salvation of the world. There is revealed to him in the Gospel the hidden truth that God's plan to save the world through Jesus Christ includes Gentiles as well as Jews. This truth simply could not be discerned by human Wisdom alone; but through the acceptance of the Gospel, and in particular, the preaching of the Gospel or 'foolishness of God', mature Christians were able to discern God's Wisdom. The mature Christian was enabled to apprehend the cosmic dimensions of the Divine Wisdom as it operated for the salvation of the whole world. From this teaching of Paul's we see how he was led to a new understanding of the meaning of Wisdom. His extension of the meaning of the term was, in a sense, forced on him by the fact of Jesus Christ. The coming of the Saviour was part of the divine purpose known only to God, and it occurred at a time judged to be in accordance with the Divine Counsel, or in Paul's phrase, in the fullness of time.

We now turn to a consideration of the other addition Paul made to the meaning of Wisdom, that is, his second use of the term, where he applies it as a category descriptive of Jesus Christ. When Paul describes Jesus as the Wisdom of God, he is pointing towards some degree of identity between Jesus Christ and Wisdom, and in this way, is providing some of the raw material for a Wisdom Christology. To appreciate the significance of this we need to recall that the figure of Wisdom, according to Judaism, stood nearer to God than anything else in the universe. By its conception of the unique proximity of Wisdom to God, Israel expressed an aspect of its understanding of the relation between God and His world. This conception affirmed two claims on behalf of Wisdom. First, Wisdom was integral to creation, in the sense that it was regarded as the intermediary, which acted as agent in God's creation of the material world. In this way, the abyss in thought between the transcendent God and the material world was bridged. Secondly, and with respect to Salvation, Wisdom bridged the gap between the Holy God and sinful man. Before Paul's time, Judaism had attained to the thought that in relation to God Creation and Salvation were to be held together. Creation and Salvation had their common source in God. But in Judaism, this was much more than an abstract theological assertion. It was part of a deeper understanding of how God dealt with the world and the men He had made. The unity of Creation and Salvation found its explanation in terms of the functions performed by Wisdom in the Divine Economy.

There are several examples of this teaching in the later Wisdom Literature. An explicit statement of the conjunction of Creation and Salvation is found in the Wisdom of Solomon:

'With thee is wisdom, who knows thy works and was present when thou didst make the world, and who understandest what is pleasing in thy sight and what is right according to thy commandments' (9:9).

The collocation of 'make the world' with 'thy commandments' should be noted. Another example worth referring to is Ecclesiasticus 24. The whole chapter is rich in its allusions to creation and salvation. It echoes reminiscences from Genesis 1, from Proverbs 8 in its account of the origin of Wisdom and also recalls the invitation Jesus gave to the weary and heavy laden. It is too long to quote but the following excerpts may be sufficient to show again how closely creation and salvation are held together in thought:

'I came forth from the mouth of the Most High, and covered the earth like a mist' (v. 3).

'Alone I have made the circuit of the vault of heaven and have walked in the depths of the abyss' (v. 5).

'Come to me, you who desire me,
and eat your fill of my produce' (v. 19).

'Whoever obeys me will not be put to shame,
and those who work with my help will not sin' (v. 22).

So far as the teaching of Paul is concerned, it is important to realize that he was not setting himself up as a Wisdom teacher anxious to reinstate Wisdom theology within current theology. Paul's writings as a whole show that although he was interested in Wisdom thought and familiar with the figure of Wisdom, yet the movement of his thought led him well beyond the frontiers normally observed by Wisdom thinkers. He breaks away from the traditional framework of their thought about Creation and Salvation and speaks of God's relations with the world in terms of Jesus Christ. The explanation of the creation of the world and the salvation of man is in terms of the historic person Jesus Christ and not the figure called Wisdom. Nevertheless, Paul sees this Jesus Christ against a background of the Wisdom tradition, for he describes Him as 'the power and wisdom of God' (1 Cor 1:24). The cosmic and redemptive functions previously associated with the figure of Wisdom are now attributed to Jesus Christ. This, of course, is an important step. It represents an understanding of the significance of Jesus in terms of a process of thought which had been characteristic of Judaism, and indeed of Israel, over many centuries. Paul has set the figure of Wisdom in a new context. Wisdom is no longer thought of in terms of a personification or a hypostasis of an attribute of God. It is now related to a person who has actually appeared in history. By his use of the category of Wisdom, Paul was able to make an appeal to those who already had some familiarity with Jewish modes of thinking, and in particular to those Gentiles who had cultural contacts with Jews of the Dispersion. References to Wisdom would remind them of their own familiar term, Word or Logos. The terms Wisdom and Word had enough in common to allow men to appreciate, in part at least, what Paul meant when he described Jesus Christ as the Wisdom of God.

It may be asked, how does Paul make the transition from the figure of Wisdom to the person of Jesus Christ? Doubtless part of the answer is that the philosophical and religious speculations of the world around him influenced his thinking. There was much coming and going intellectually among thinkers, who nowadays are conveniently, if not accurately, classified under such general titles as Gnostic or Hellenistic or Jewish. But so far as Paul's interest in the cosmic significance of Jesus Christ is concerned, there is no need to range far and wide. For within Judaism and Christianity there were ideas and terms at least as adequate as any to be found elsewhere. Although Paul aimed at propounding an explanation of the cosmic significance of Jesus Christ, he was not indulging in speculation in the interest of theory alone. Rather he was claiming that the personal experience of salvation, vouchsafed to him and his fellow-Christians, demanded that they think of Jesus Christ as the unique mediator between God and the world, including mankind. For Paul, as well as for the authors of the

Prologue to John's Gospel and the opening verses of the Epistle to the Hebrews, the long tradition of Jewish Wisdom teaching with all its developments, lay close at hand. In its later developments, the figure of Wisdom had come to be regarded as of cosmic import; also, it possessed pre-existence; it was uniquely associated with the Creation; it showed man the way to Salvation.

Paul takes up these ideas and integrates them into his teaching about the person of Jesus Christ. Nevertheless, it is no general or wholesale transfer of what first belonged to Wisdom, to the person of Jesus Christ. There were two attributes which seemed to him important: the place of Wisdom in Creation and its place in Salvation. These seemed significant to him because they were involved in the experience Paul and his fellow-Christians had of the power of Jesus Christ (cf. Rom 1:16). To appreciate the significance of this, it will be necessary to digress from our hitherto direct discussion of Paul's teaching. Our starting-point in the digression is a consideration of a too readily overlooked element in the work of Jesus, viz. Jesus as Teacher.

The first Christians recognized in Jesus a great teacher. He was not only comparable with Moses but uniquely greater. The Law, or to use a better term, the Torah, was traditionally ascribed to Moses. But the Sermon on the Mount, as given by Jesus, was regarded as displacing the traditional Torah. A Christian comment on this claim is provided in John's Gospel: 'For the law was given through Moses; grace and truth came through Jesus Christ' (1:17). The brief passage, Mark I: 21–28, also shows how the teaching of Jesus was regarded as a break away from the dominance of the Torah of Moses. Mark records the reaction of the people to the new Teacher. 'They were astonished at his teaching.' His 'authority' set him apart from all other teachers. The onlookers called out, 'What is this? A new teaching!' This early tradition, preserved in the gospel records, supplies Paul with evidence that Jesus the Teacher held a more central place in the divine economy than ever Moses did, in his relation to the Torah given on Sinai. In the words of W. D. Davies,[1] 'It is possible to infer from this the important consequence that not only did the words of Jesus form a Torah for Paul, but so also did the person of Jesus. In a real sense conformity to Christ, His teaching and His life, has taken the place of conformity to the Jewish Torah. Jesus Himself—in word and deed or fact is a new Torah.'

An interesting supplement to this view comes from the Jewish scholar, Joseph Klausner,[2] 'The Torah of Israel, with all its regulations, was null and void. What came to take its place, besides the two ceremonial practices just mentioned (baptism and the Lord's Supper)? The answer to this question is brief: *faith in Christ.*' Klausner, of course, dissents from the statement just quoted. But he too agrees that Paul taught that Jesus took the place of the Torah of the Old Testament.

Paul's point is that what the written Torah had failed to do has now become possible through this person Jesus Christ, who can be described as the New Torah. By identifying Jesus with the Torah, Paul is doing something parallel with what Judaism did when it identified Wisdom and Torah. This identification finds clear expression in Ecclesiasticus, but it can be traced back to an earlier period. The Old Testament is a source for the view that the Torah is the written form which the Divine Wisdom takes. In Deut 4:6, the Israelites are commanded to observe the 'statutes and ordinances', because, 'that

---

[1] *Paul and Rabbinic Judaism*, p. 148.
[2] *From Jesus to Paul*, p. 516, italics original.

will be your wisdom'. A more developed expression is
given in Ecclesiasticus 24. Wisdom, we are told, lived in
its 'dwelling in Jacob', received Israel as an inheritance,
ministered in the tabernacle, was established in Zion and
dwelt in Jerusalem. With such views as these for his
background, Paul was fully familiar with the exalted
status of Wisdom in the eyes of Judaism. It will have
been noticed how closely some of the utterances about
the Torah resemble what Paul says about Jesus Christ.
Some further references, recorded in literature a little
later than Paul's date, point back, however, to a tendency
to exalt Torah which had been at work even before his
time. We refer to some of the teaching of Rabbinic
Judaism. There it is taught that God spends three hours
daily in the study of Torah, that the Messiah too studies
it, and indeed will make no addition to it when he comes.
C. G. Montefiore[1] says of the Torah, 'It seems to have
some sort of independent and cosmic existence, even as
its creation took place long before the creation of man',
and elsewhere in the same volume[2] adds, 'I think, we
must admit, most truly of all, God created the world for
the sake of the Torah or for the sake of Israel . . .'. It is
not surprising, in the light of this kind of language, that
the Torah is conceived of as interceding for Israel and as
being personified.[3] Also, the Torah was in being before
creation in that it existed for a thousand generations
prior to the Creation.[4]

However necessary it is to make allowances for poetic
fancy and the warmth of personal devotion, it will be
agreed that this is the kind of thought-world with which
Paul would be familiar. This identification of Wisdom
and Torah is a development which continued long in

---

[1] In *A Rabbinic Anthology*, edd, Montefiore and Loewe, p. xxxiii.
[2] *Ib.* p. 37.   [3] *Ib.* p. 677.   [4] *Ib.* p. 169.

Israel. As early as the book of Proverbs, the wise man was identified with the righteous.[1] Also, as a parallel process, if not indeed part of the same process, Judaism sought to make Wisdom ever more Jewish and to regard it as Israel's own peculiar contribution towards man's understanding of the relations between God and the world. But the cosmopolitan and international element in Wisdom itself exerted an influence too, in that it tended to regard the Torah as being nearer to man as man or Gentile, and less exclusively for the Jew alone. 'God's Torah, like Wisdom, becomes a universal law. . . . The law is no longer, as in the O.T., the rule of life for those belonging to the chosen people. . . . It is now the timeless expression of the divine will with a validity of its own.'[2]

After the above digression, it may be easier to see how Paul approached the question of the Person of Jesus Christ by regarding Him as the personal and incarnate expression of the Torah, indeed, as a New Torah. In Paul's view, Jesus is the new bearer of attributes formerly ascribed to Torah. The Old Torah recedes into the background; it has served its purpose; it was 'but a shadow of the good things to come' (Heb 10:4), 'our custodian until Christ came' (Gal 3:24f); it has been replaced by Jesus Christ. There is no need for Paul to go outside the developed tradition of Judaism into which he had been born, nor outside the Christian tradition into which he had entered, in order to find categories capable of explaining the unique and supreme status of Jesus Christ. The raw materials for thinking in cosmic terms about this Jesus Christ, who had come to Paul as a revelation from God, were drawn to a considerable extent from the stock-

[1] Cf. *Law* by Kleinknecht and Gutbrod, p. 55.
[2] *Ib.* p. 56.

in-trade of Wisdom thought. The most obvious point at which Paul availed himself of the Wisdom tradition was in connection with Creation and Salvation. Whereas at one stage in the course of the divine revelation in Israel, the Torah had been the connecting link with Creation and Salvation, now, in the fullness of time, these are to be explained in terms of Jesus Christ, the New Torah, or, in Paul's phrase, 'the power of God and the wisdom of God'.

It may be useful to close by summarizing the diverse elements which can be traced in Paul's teaching on Wisdom. He shares in much of the current teaching on the subject. It is, at one level, a human attribute, but of course has its source in God. There is also a divine Wisdom. This is distinct from the human, in that it is mysterious, secret and exclusive to God. Despite this, some truths of the divine Wisdom are made available to certain Christians, that is, to those who are said to be mature. It is imparted to them as a blessing which accompanies the acceptance of the Gospel. There is a third use of Wisdom to which Paul draws attention. It is an epithet applied solely to Jesus Christ but which seems to be something more than merely a descriptive term. Paul applies it in connection with certain functions more usually associated with the figure of Wisdom. In particular, he connects with Jesus Christ the powers to create the world and to save mankind. Such powers, before Jesus Christ, had been attributed either to Wisdom or to the Torah. Teaching of this kind by Paul about powers exercised by Jesus Christ leads quite naturally to questions about the Person of our Lord and to a consideration of some of the aspects of a Wisdom Christology.

X.—TOWARDS A CHRISTOLOGY

At an early stage in our Lord's ministry, He asked His followers the question, 'Who do men say that I am? (Mark 8:27). The answer was given by Peter: 'You are the Christ'. It is the answer of faith to the question about the Person of Jesus Christ. It asserts that Jesus was divine in a way that could be said of no other human being. But, of course, it is not the only answer provided by the New Testament, even if the other answers are largely commentary on it. Paul, and the authors of the Fourth Gospel, and the Epistle to Hebrews, to name but three, have attempted to express their deepest thoughts about Jesus Christ. Quite a number of titles have been applied to Him. Some, indeed, were used by Jesus of Himself, such as Son of Man. His followers called Him Lord. The title Son of God was applied by Satan, and by demoniacs, and was used indirectly by Jesus Himself in the parable of the Wicked Husbandmen. This last title, Son of God, is obviously Christological, in the sense that it makes a specific claim about the person of Jesus. It says, in effect, who He is. There are several titles with this significance. One of the best known, although not the most frequently used, is 'The Word'. Others are 'The Image of God', 'The First Born', 'The Last Adam'. The one which most concerns us in this chapter is 'The Wisdom of God'. We shall try to find out what this title, and the thoughts and ideas associated with it, tell us about His person. What truths about Him does it point

to, truths which are necessary to our appreciation of
what the first Christians believed about Him? We have
to admit that the New Testament does not provide sufficient data for the formulation of what can strictly be
called a Wisdom Christology, at all comparable with
what can be called a Johannine Christology or a Pauline
one. It is true, of course, that what is regarded as consti-
tuting a Wisdom Christology is very much a matter of
definition of terms. But as we are not engaged in writing
a Christology, we shall attempt a much humbler task.
We shall try to get as clear an understanding as possible
of the Person of Jesus Christ as seen from the point of
view of such Wisdom thought as is found in the New
Testament.

Our previous consideration of the place of Wisdom in
Paul's thought has emphasized two truths about the
significance of Jesus Christ. The first is His status in the
work of man's salvation or, more comprehensively, of
the salvation of the whole world; the second is His place
in the creation of the universe. The mere statement of
these views about Jesus reminds us that there must have
been a certain amount of cosmological thinking among
Christians at an early stage in their reflections on Jesus
Christ. This was not due solely to intellectual and speculative interests. More probably it arose from a necessity
inseparable from the religious evaluation Christians
made of Jesus Christ, based on what had happened
within their own experiences. Through the effects of the
life and teaching of Jesus, and as a result of His resur-
rection from the dead, the Church had come to a new
understanding of God, the world, man himself, and inseparable from these, a new understanding of this person,
Jesus Christ. He was central and essential to the new
thinking forced upon them. However much their thinking

tried to express itself in language borrowed from current theology and philosophy; however much influences from Gnosticism, Hellenism and even Judaism tended to shape their formulas about the Person of Jesus Christ, nevertheless there was a religious impetus, or rather a religious inspiration, also at work. The religious experience, with its source in Jesus Christ, gave power to the movement of thought about His person and, no less, this experience exercised some control over those dangers which might arise from the more speculative interests. There was always the danger, as Paul demonstrates in First Corinthians, that there could be a confusion between what Christians had learned in their experience of Jesus Christ, with speculations which arose, as Paul puts it, from 'a wisdom of this age or of the rulers of this age' (I Cor 2:6).

At least three writers in the New Testament attempt to formulate a Christology which uses terms and thoughts closely related to Wisdom theology. They are Paul, the author of the Epistle to the Hebrews, and the writer of the Prologue to John's Gospel. If some of Paul's epistles, or parts of them, are to be ascribed to a later writer, who shared his thoughts and could be technically named a 'Paulinist', then we may have to reckon the number as four (or more). But for our purposes, it is not necessary to distinguish between Paul personally and some other unnamed writer who, presumably, was influenced by him. In particular, it is possible to argue that part, but not all, of the Epistle to the Colossians is by a Paulinist rather than by Paul; but a decision on this question is not required here. More important for our purposes is the question whether Jesus regarded Himself as personified Wisdom. In our earlier discussion, in chapter VIII, we gave a negative answer to that question. Yet, at the same time, we should bear in mind the incontrovertible fact that Jesus drew attention to parallels between the figure of Wisdom and Himself. He made numerous references to Wisdom, used its vocabulary and followed its methods in His teaching, with the result that it was all but psychologically inevitable that some of His followers would approach the question of His person along the lines of thought characteristic of Wisdom. For several centuries before Jesus, many religious thinkers, in Israel and outside too, had sought to trace a connection between the figure of Wisdom and God. Wisdom had come to be accepted as a category capable of being used to explain the relation of God to the creation of the world and the salvation of mankind.

A sufficient account of this subject has already been provided; all that need be done at this stage is to recall some of the factors which operated in Wisdom thought. Wisdom, it will be remembered, stood in a uniquely intimate relationship to God. It performed specific functions in creation; it offered a way of life that led to salvation, seen particularly in the identification of Torah and Wisdom. Claims like these when made on behalf of Wisdom would rouse echoes in the minds of Christians so long as they continued to reflect on the mystery of the Person of their Lord. This comes out clearly in Paul, in particular. His earlier education, his familiarity with rabbinic modes of thought and argument, his personal experience of the Risen Christ and his encounter with Jewish and Hellenistic speculations within the churches he evangelized, led him to reflect on the Person of Jesus Christ. In one of the many strands of his thinking he reflected on the relation there might be between the speculative figure of Wisdom and the historical figure, Jesus Christ. But we must not commit the error of imagining

that Paul was alone in thinking about Jesus Christ in this
way. Indeed, he was not even an innovator in writing
about Him in terms of Wisdom. Paul was not the first to
reflect on the Person of his Lord; he had entered a
tradition on the subject, to which, of course, he made his
own contribution.

In this connection, the striking passage, Matt 11:25–30
is significant. It may be that not all the words in this
passage ascribed to Jesus are His *ipsissima verba*; much
or some is due to the influence of early followers of Jesus.
But if this be so, have we not then good evidence to
suggest that others, as well as Paul, were finding Wisdom
categories helpful towards an understanding of Jesus
Christ? Further, as will be shown later in this chapter,
the Prologue to John's Gospel and the opening verses of
Hebrews use language descriptive of Jesus Christ which
belong to the Wisdom ways of thought. An approach to
Christology along the lines of Wisdom is not really a
deviation or an eccentricity introduced, as it were, by a
speculative aberration on the part of Paul. On the contrary, it was a way of thinking about Jesus Christ which
seemed eminently natural and reasonable to the first
Christians. It helped to clarify their minds on the ever-
recurring questions of God's relations to the world He
had created, and how men were to be saved. As indicated
earlier in this chapter, largely because Jesus Christ had
come, men were forced into new thinking about God, the
world and human destiny. The New Testament, as one
part of its wider presentation of its Lord to the Jewish-
Hellenistic world, spoke of Him as that unique person,
in whom the Creation found its origin and explanation,
and who alone was the sole mediator of God's salvation
of mankind.

There were, of course, other influences of a less speculative nature at work, which had a connection with Wisdom. For example, Paul found in the church at Corinth that there were people associated with the congregation who were making a quite improper use of the term Wisdom. He had the task of setting any discussion of Wisdom into a Christian context, and, as it were, to embed it in a foundation of 'righteousness and sanctification and redemption' (I Cor 1:30). Also, the Prologue to John's Gospel, although it does not use the term Wisdom, but Word, seeks to anchor what it has to say on the subject in the fact of the Incarnation. Over against all speculation, legitimate or otherwise, it declares that the Word became flesh (1:14). Further, the opening verses of Hebrews seek to repel any speculation which would detract from the unique, exalted supremacy of Jesus Christ. Indeed, these verses exalt Him above angels and Moses. So far as Christological interests are involved, it seems fairly evident that an examination of Wisdom may lead us towards a deeper understanding of what the New Testament teaches about the person of Jesus Christ.

When we turn to the New Testament, it is worth noticing the rather varied vocabulary, based on Wisdom, which is employed. The person of Jesus Christ is variously described as 'image', 'firstborn', 'power and wisdom', and these are employed in connection with creation and salvation. Three passages in particular call for discussion, as having a quite clearly defined relation to Wisdom thought; they are (*a*) Colossians 1:15–22, (*b*) Hebrews 1:1–4, (*c*) John 1:1–18. Of other passages the most important is I Cor 8:6, and we propose to begin with it.

The relevant words are: '. . . and one Lord, Jesus Christ, through whom are all things and through whom we exist'. As a comment on this, we draw attention to the paraphrase of it made by Robertson and Plummer, in their Commentary on I Corinthians.[1] They write, '. . . and but one Lord, Jesus Christ, through whom the whole universe was made and through whom we were made anew'. This paraphrase, we suggest, provides the setting for Paul's statement within the then current framework of Wisdom thought. It is important to observe the collocation of creation and redemption as attributed to the power of Jesus Christ. The occasion for the utterance is one on which Paul has been at pains to repudiate the existence of 'idols', 'so-called gods', 'gods' and 'lords'. Over against the speculative theology of those under the influence of false knowledge, Paul declares there is only one God, the Father, and alongside that statement he joins certain special claims on behalf of Jesus Christ. The phrase 'through whom' demands attention. It occurs twice. The first indicates the work of Jesus Christ in creation; the second occurrence points to the new creation of mankind made possible through Jesus Christ. Bultmann[2] says this verse is 'a formula in which the cosmological and the soteriological roles of Christ are combined. He points out that this cosmic and mediatorial role is introduced in so matter-of-fact a manner that it seems to be a view which Paul shared with others. But apart from such support as Bultmann may be able to give to our point of view, Paul's words themselves remind us of the quite similar roles traditionally ascribed to Wisdom. However, what is of no less importance is that he leaves the Corinthians in no doubt that the Father and the Son are one in creation and salvation. This quite fundamental presupposition is basic to any proper understanding of how the categories of Wisdom are relevant to the person of Jesus Christ.

The second passage, Colossians 1:15–29, penetrates

---

[1] I.C.C., p. 162. [2] *Theology of the New Testament*, p. 132.

much further into our subject. Whether written by Paul
or a Paulinist (although it is difficult to think of an unnamed follower making so remarkable a contribution),
the emphasis is clearly on the cosmological significance
of our Lord. This great Christological utterance regards
Jesus Christ as supreme over all created things. He is the
image of God and everything is held in being by Him
and finds its place in the cosmos in relation to Him. 'He
is the image of the invisible God, the first-born of all
creation; for in him all things were created, . . . all things
were created through him and for him. He is before all
things, and in him all things hold together. . . . For in
him all the fullness of God was pleased to dwell, and
through him to reconcile to himself all things' (Col
1:15–20).

Again we note how uniquely Jesus Christ is at one with
the Father in the works of creation and redemption. The
passage itself is heavily loaded with technical terms.
Some would trace them back to the Wisdom vocabulary.
Others, in particular Bultmann, would look to a Gnostic
source. But even Bultmann is prepared to admit that the
passage has been adapted to suit the Christian point of
view. He says of it that it is 'a hymn which the author
has rather strongly accommodated to the Christian
tradition by his editing of it"[1] However, the earlier
verses, at least vv. 15–18, are not only more probably
derived from Wisdom, but also are more readily understood on the basis of such a derivation. For example, 'the
image of the invisible God'. The word for 'image' is the
same as the one used in the Wisdom of Solomon (7:26)
in the phrase, 'the image of his goodness'. It also recalls
the Old Testament creation narrative, at Gen 1:27: 'God
created man in his own image', and Paul's words at

[1] *Ib.* p. 176.

2 Cor 4:4, where it is translated as 'likeness', with reference to Christ, 'who is the likeness of God'. It seems unnecessary to invoke Gnostic influences to the extent of neglecting the Old Testament and Wisdom usage, especially when these lie so close at hand in the life of Paul and his fellow Christians.

We meet with the same modes of thinking about Jesus Christ in that other phrase, 'first-born of all creation'. Here again attention is called to a characteristic of Wisdom, namely its existence before any other creature. Traditionally, Wisdom enjoyed a lengthy, aristocratic pedigree, going back to before the beginning of creation. Here in Colossians the writer claims not only priority in time before anything that has been created but also that Jesus Christ is distinct and separate from the genus of creature. He is not a created entity at all. As the following verse puts it, 'for in him all things were created in heaven and on earth, visible and invisible, whether thrones or dominions or principalities or authorities—all things were created through him and for him'. In other words, Jesus Christ is the active agent in creation and in no sense a part of creation.

The theme of Christ's priority in time, or pre-existence, to the creation is emphasized in v. 17, in the words, 'He is before all things'. This is appropriate from the Old Testament point of view where a superior status was accorded to the first-born. Here it points to the unique dignity Jesus Christ possesses, which sets Him apart from the creation. Further, the second part of the verse, 'in him all things hold together', claims that the creation finds its place and meaning in Him and not in itself. He is the principle, if so abstract a term be permitted, which gives unity to the creation and makes it a true cosmos. Jesus Christ is regarded as supreme over all created beings, whether men or angels or other powers. But His pre-eminence is not only cosmological, it is also soteriological. It is not limited to the creation of the universe; it extends also to the salvation of mankind, and indeed to everything in the created order. His unique, pre-existent oneness with the Father is the source of His power to redeem. 'For in him all the fulness of God was pleased to dwell, and through him to reconcile to himself all things, whether on earth or in heaven, making peace by the blood of his cross' (vv. 19, 20). The salvation effected by Jesus is cosmic and inclusive of the whole creation, and He alone is sufficient for so universal a task because the fullness of God is in Him alone.

The language used here finds several important parallels in Wisdom thought. Just as it was taught in later Judaism that God was, in some sense, in Wisdom, so now in the New Testament it is claimed that the fullness of God dwells in Jesus Christ. But there is one fundamental difference. This is clearly expressed in Col 2:9, 'For in him the whole fullness of deity dwells bodily'. Judaism had taught that Wisdom had made its abode in Israel and had tabernacled there, but in Christianity the Divine Wisdom resides in Jesus Christ, that is, in a historic person, as distinct from an ideal or hypostasized figure. Jesus is accorded unique and divine status. Inseparable from this exalted rank are two characteristics, (*a*) His superiority over the whole created order which He brought into being, and (*b*) His divinely bestowed power from the Father to effect the salvation of the world. The noteworthy feature is that these claims on behalf of Jesus Christ are expressed in terms otherwise applied to the figure of Wisdom.

A similar use of Wisdom terminology and ideas appears in the next passage, Hebrews 1:1–4. Although the

particular term 'Wisdom' is not used, nevertheless the
ideas and thoughts associated with the term are clearly represented. Jesus Christ is regarded as God's Son. He is
pre-eminent over all creatures, including angels. He created
the world. He upholds 'the universe by his word of
power' (v. 3). Further, 'he made purification for sins'
(v. 4). Here again we find the collocation of Creation and
Redemption in relation to Jesus Christ. His pre-eminence
over all created things and beings is spoken of in terms
of Wisdom and recalls Prov 8:22f. Further, the phrase
'reflects the glory of God' is the same word as is used in
Wisdom of Solomon 7:26, which is translated as 'reflection of eternal light'. The opening verses, too, are followed
by a series of quotations, vv. 10–12, which, among other
things, draw attention to the Son's part in creation. The
author is pointing back to a pre-existent Christ who is
with God prior to Creation. In this view, Hebrews is in
agreement with Paul and John. Like them, his endeavour
to articulate the significance of the person of Jesus Christ
was done by the utilization of categories provided
already by Wisdom teaching. There was, of course, one
important difference at this point between the New
Testament and Wisdom Literature. Whereas Proverbs
8:22f, Wisdom of Solomon 7:22f, and Ecclesiasticus 24:1f,
are referring to an hypostasized or an abstract figure,
the New Testament writers refer to an historic person.

In the last passage, John 1:1–18, this emphasis upon a
historic person is, if possible, more emphatic, and the
reference to Wisdom modes of thought is no less clear.
The opening words, 'In the beginning', recall Gen 1:1,
and the term 'beginning' itself is a well-established phrase
in Wisdom. Prov 8:22f uses 'beginning' to indicate that
Wisdom was with God before the creation. Here Proverbs
is dependent on Gen 1:1, as is John 1:1. Further, the idea

of 'beginning' as it is expressed in Proverbs is continued in Wisdom writings, in the Wisdom of Solomon, and, to a lesser extent, in Ecclesiasticus. This continuation of a specific term is part of a wider interconnection between the Prologue of John and Wisdom thought. Several parallels between the Wisdom of Solomon and the Prologue will illustrate this, and can be set out as follows: (We have arranged them alternately, i.e. the quotation from John is given in the line (*a*), and refers, of course, to Jesus Christ, and the quotation from the Wisdom of Solomon is given at (*b*) and refers to the figure of Wisdom.)

1 (*a*) 1:3. 'All things were made through him'.
   (*b*) 7:22. 'Wisdom the fashioner of all things'. (Cf. 8:6.)

2 (*a*) 1:5. 'the light shines'.
   (*b*) 6:12. 'radiant and unfading'.

3 (*a*) 1:5. 'the darkness has not overcome it'.
   (*b*) 6:29. 'compared with the light she is found to be superior'.

4 (*a*) 1:9. 'the true light'.
   (*b*) 7:10. 'I chose to have her rather than light'.

5 (*a*) 1:12. 'he gave power to become children of God'.
   (*b*) 7:27. 'make them friends of God'.

6 (*a*) 1:14. 'glory as of the only[1] Son from the Father'.
   (*b*) 7:25. 'a pure emanation of the glory of the Almighty'.

Further confirmation of the close relation between the Prologue and Wisdom is found in Ecclesiasticus. In

[1] The word translated ' only Son ' in John 1:14, sometimes translated ' only begotten ', is the same as the word used in Wisdom of Solomon and translated as ' unique '. It can also be translated in a sense nearer to the term ' first-born ' as found in Col. 1:15.

F

Ecclus 24, vv. 4 and 8, Wisdom is identified with Law, and significantly regarded as the perfect expression of divine Wisdom. The important phrases are, 'I dwell', 'pillar of cloud', 'make your dwelling'. This kind of language refers to God's dwelling in Israel, God's glory and the divine revelation. Similarly, in the Prologue the context is one in which the glory of Christ is proclaimed, His superiority over Moses and the Law affirmed and the divine revelation in the Son proclaimed. What in the Wisdom literature had been ascribed to the figure of Wisdom has now been taken up into the person and functions of the Son or Word (cf. John 1:14, 17, 18). In Ecclus 42:15, God is praised as Creator, 'By the words of the Lord his works are done'; this should be compared with John 1:3. Ecclus 43:26, 'by his word all things hold together', and 43:33, 'the Lord has made all things, and to the godly he has granted wisdom', should be compared with John 1:3, 10. The language of 43:26 recalls Col 1:17, with its 'in him all things hold together'. Although the Greek in Ecclesiasticus and Colossians only resemble one another and are not identical, yet both writers are in agreement with John in bringing Wisdom thought about Creation into relations with Jesus Christ.

We must resist the temptation either to over-simplify the relation between the Prologue and Wisdom Literature by making too much of literary resemblances, or to claim an undue precision in the relations between them; yet it cannot be denied that John avails himself of Wisdom in his own efforts to ascribe cosmic functions to Jesus Christ. In so doing, John is aligning himself with the two other writers we have discussed, Paul and Hebrews. This joint agreement on the part of three so independent writers is as good evidence as can properly be asked for, to lead to the conclusion that the data for a

Wisdom Christology go back to a rather early period in Christian thinking. The manner of their presentation of the data suggests that what they were discussing were generally accepted conclusions and not a novelty nor an innovation introduced as their private or personal discovery.

Perhaps enough has been already said to show that Wisdom thought contributed to a deeper understanding of the mystery of the Person of Jesus Christ. In particular, it confirmed the claim that this Jesus Christ, whom they had found in experience to be their Saviour, was also the unique Son of God Who was the divine agent in the Creation. But Wisdom thought enabled Christians to go further. It led them to see that this universe had been made in accordance with the Divine Wisdom, that it was a rational and reasonable whole. Its meaning could be discerned by the employment of the God-given Wisdom made available to man. Christian thinkers such as Paul, the author of Hebrews, and John followed the clue offered by Wisdom thought and claimed that the partial truth discerned in the figure of Wisdom was revealed in its completion in the person of Jesus Christ. 'All things were created through him and for him. He is before all things, and in him all things hold together' (Col 1:16, 17). The universe finds its meaning and also its purpose in Jesus Christ. The Prologue says the same but in a different way. But John goes beyond Wisdom thought when he declares that the Word became flesh. This is not at all a continuation of Wisdom, it is something really new. The unique, divine Agent of Creation had condescended to become part of the very creation He had made. It is at this point that the divine revelation reaches its finality. For it is just here that the purpose of the created universe is revealed, and also, what the possibilities of human life are on earth. To be more specific, this purpose is now seen to be identical with the purpose which led to the Creation taking place in the first instance or 'in the beginning'. The possibilities of human life are now seen in the life lived by the Son of God or Word, on earth. The world no longer required to speculate about an ideal figure, the reality had now come, and the Word became flesh and dwelt among us.

In conclusion, it should be recalled that we have already expressed doubt that the New Testament provides a completed Wisdom Christology. We have to avoid reading our later ideas, especially those developed in the Christological debates of later centuries, into the New Testament data. Paul, Hebrews and John used traditional language, which sometimes was poetic and often slightly vague. We must not try to be more precise than they would have wished. Yet, we must not be too cavalier, and dismiss what they write as if their handling of the available data made no significant contribution to Christology. Each one of these, in his own way, was led along the pathway of Wisdom thought to insights into the truth about Jesus Christ in relation to the creation of the Universe and the Salvation of Mankind. They were led to make claims of a cosmic kind. Not only was Jesus Christ the Creator and Saviour; in Him these two claims were united and integrated. Salvation is assured because He who is the Creator of the world is its Saviour. The Creator Himself is no creature but the divine, pre-existent Son of God. The Wisdom which was with God in the beginning has in the Son or Word of God become flesh, and dwelt among us, full of grace and truth.

APPENDIX I

HYPOSTASIS IN RELATION TO WISDOM

THE later use of the term hypostasis in the controversies about the relations between the three persons in the Blessed Trinity does not concern us in this work. In any case the term in the doctrine of the Trinity has its own peculiar connotation. Also, the possibility that there may be hypostases other than that related to the Wisdom hypostasis does not concern us.

The meaning of hypostasis in relation to Wisdom is notoriously difficult. The dictionaries do not assist much but they show the wide range of meaning of the term. Those relevant here include 'existence', 'reality', 'essence', and 'personality'. The metaphorical use draws attention to 'that which underlies a thing', or 'its substance'. In the more theological use it indicates either 'personality' or 'personal existence' or 'person'. No additional light is cast on its meaning by the two associated verbs, 'hypostasize' and 'hypostatize'.

In its Greek form, ὑπόστασις is a feminine noun. It is used in Wisdom of Solomon 16:21, in the phrase, 'Thy sustenance manifested thy sweetness toward thy children'. The reference is to the miracle of the provision of manna in the wilderness. This miracle of manna manifested the divine nature, or more literally, the substance of the divine nature. The truth behind this use of hypostasis is that the manna, in its visible, material form, is a

F*

manifestation of the invisible God. Further, at 7:25, 26 the writer seems to be saying that Wisdom possesses divinity but is not deity. Yet, at the same time, Wisdom is not just a thing, nor a mere attribute of God. It is much more complex than an attribute. It behaves rather like a person who has several attributes. It enters into personal relations with men and seems to have the qualities of a person, and exercises such qualities in accordance with directions laid down by God. Drummond[1] says, 'we shall not go far astray if we venture to sum up our author's view on this point in the brief statement that Wisdom is personal, but not a person'. This is an attractive view. It emphasizes the personal element in Wisdom without committing anyone to saying that Wisdom is a person.

In the New Testament there are several occurrences of hypostasis, 2 Cor 9:14; 11:17 and Heb 1:3, 3:14 and 11:1. All but Heb 1:3 move towards the meaning of 'confidence' and associate it with Christian hope. The translation of Heb 1:3 is 'the very stamp of his nature', hypostasis being translated as 'nature'. It means here, the being or essence of God. It sheds only a little light on the subject in that it points to the Divine nature rather than to man.

From the above it will be seen that precision in the use of the term hypostasis is an ideal to be aimed at rather than an achieved fact. This is borne out by the most comprehensive modern treatment of the subject, that of Helmer Ringgren, *Word and Wisdom*. He gives it the sub-title, 'Studies in the Hypostatization of Divine Qualities and Functions in the Ancient Near East'. He writes, 'It would be convenient to establish from the outset what we mean by a "hypostasis". For it has become evident, e.g. in the discussion about personified

[1] *Philo Judaeus*, Vol. I, p. 226.

Wisdom in the O.T., that the difference of opinion as to whether Wisdom is a hypostasis or not is due to the fact that different scholars have worked with different definitions of the concept "hypostasis".[1] He himself prefers a wider definition and thinks of it as a 'quasi-personification of certain attributes proper to God, occupying an intermediate position between personalities and abstract beings.'

This attractive view, however, seems to lead to the conclusion that there is no agreed definition of hypostasis. The most we can hope for are certain broad generalizations or, better, some guiding criteria which may control the data at our disposal. We hope to develop this latter view about criteria at the end of this appendix. The best approach to the problem is to regard Wisdom as a special example of hypostasis. A consideration of the history of the term Wisdom is helpful in this connection. Wisdom came to be regarded by human thought as something richer and more complex than a personification of an attribute. It may well be that Wisdom began its career, if we may so put it, as a Divine attribute which man personified. But it underwent a development, which differentiated it from other attributes. It came to be set over against God, although under His control. It became His agent and was said to enjoy His presence or company. By this process of accretion, as it were, Wisdom moved away from the category of personification. But that is not the end of its development. It came to possess sufficient powers of attraction to draw to itself the characteristics of sex and was regarded as a female. It was described as a gracious woman, a hostess, a bride, a wife, even a preacher. Much of this language is poetic and metaphorical. But even so, such a complex entity, with

[1] *Op. cit.*, p. 8.

so many concrete features, and regarded as performing so many technical functions, can hardly be called simply a personification. In actual usage Wisdom has a special status in the realm of thought. It is an instrument used for the articulation of the relations between God and His universe, including even the realms of Creation and Redemption. Because of claims such as these, there seems to be justification for describing Wisdom by such a term as hypostasis.

Although we propose to classify Wisdom as a hypostasis, we admit that this still leaves a number of unanswered questions about its status in reality. First, there is the problem hinted at by Drummond, in the subtle distinction he drew between Wisdom as 'a person' and as 'personal'. However attractive the distinction may be, it seems to be based on a literary *tour de force*, rather than on an examination of the usage of the term Wisdom itself; it is verbal rather than concrete. But the element of truth in Drummond's dictum is that it reminds us that this is the kind of question (i.e. 'person' versus 'personal') which a hypostasis is bound to raise, just because it is a hypostasis. This suggests to us a useful criterion for judging whether an entity like Wisdom is a hypostasis or not. It should, on account of the functions ascribed to it, raise in the minds of men the question of its status in reality. In the case of Wisdom, it is clear that it cannot claim to be a person in the sense that a human being is a person. Yet, it functions and behaves in a way which can be described as personal. Judged by this criterion Wisdom is to be called a hypostasis.

A second criterion we should commend is that of its place in the divine economy. Wisdom is of significance for human thought in that it is engaged in activities of a cosmic kind. It is connected with the divine action in

Creation and Salvation. Its contribution within the cosmic sphere arises from within the purposes of God rather than from the purposes of man. In this sense Wisdom mediates between God and His world. This claim on behalf of Wisdom is in favour of calling it a hypostasis.

A possible third criterion is based on a practical distinction we should like to draw between a personification and a hypostasis. A personification tends to be simple and to be limited to just one attribute taken in separation from other attributes. Its affinities tend also to be literary. So far as hypostasis is concerned with Wisdom, the later history of Wisdom shows an increasing complexity of its characteristics. The recognition of this fact demands that the difference between personification and hypostasis be observed, at least for the later developments of Wisdom. On this basis, Wisdom is to be regarded as a hypostasis. Whatever be the number of criteria deemed necessary for classifying an entity as a hypostasis, it is important that they should be derived from the concrete characteristics of that entity as these are manifested in man's thinking about it. On this basis, therefore we conclude that Wisdom is best treated as a hypostasis.

WISDOM AND THE VIRGIN MARY

In the last hundred years or so, there has been a great growth in interest in the Virgin Mary. The two most significant dates in that period are 1854, when the Immaculate Conception of Mary was officially proclaimed by the Roman Catholic Church, and 1950, when the Dogma of her Assumption was accepted. Such developments in popular piety and theological study raise questions about the relation of the Virgin Mary to Christian thought about Wisdom. Many within the Roman Catholic Church seem to find no difficulty in identifying Mary with Wisdom.

There has been a continuous popular demand for the presence of what might be called a 'feminine' element in the Godhead. Some critics of this demand allege that the functions previously exercised by pagan mother-deities, like Isis, Minerva and Cybele have infiltrated into Christianity. This suggestion gains plausibility, so far as these three goddesses are concerned, in that in addition to being female mother-goddesses, they were also renowned for their Wisdom. There is also the interesting grammatical fact that the word 'Wisdom', both in Greek and in Hebrew is of feminine gender. It is suggested that elements like these, when taken together, would facilitate a correlation of Wisdom with the Virgin Mary. Another possible factor is that religion looks to theology for enlightenment about the nature of a suitable mediator between God and man. The need for a mediator is always present and, indeed, the quality of a religion may well be judged by the kind of mediator it proclaims. Wisdom in an obvious sense possessed many of the attributes of a mediator. So far as the Virgin Mary is concerned, at a date as late as the fifth century A.D., there was a discernible tendency towards a cult of Mary, which regarded her as possessing mediatorial qualities.

Within the last century, more emphasis has been placed upon Mary as an intermediary between man and God. Indeed, some Roman Catholic authorities suggest that Mariology has trespassed on those areas normally reserved for Christology and Pneumatology. It is inevitable in these days when so much is being written about the Virgin Mary, that there should be much that is theologically doubtful. Fortunately there are scholars, not confined to any one branch of the Christian Church, who are aware of the serious nature of the problem and who are exercised as to how best to bring a sober judgement to bear upon a subject in which emotions are easily aroused. We propose, therefore, to cast a brief glance at three works which may be accepted as being significant in relation to Mariology. The first is a symposium *The Blessed Virgin Mary: Essays by Anglicans*, edited by Mascall and Box (1963). The aim of the work as stated by the editors in their preface is to 'bear witness to a common conviction on the part of a number of Anglicans, namely that the Blessed Mother of the Lord has been badly neglected in recent Anglican theology and that, for the sake of the Anglican Communion and of Christendom as a whole, it is desirable that this neglect should be corrected'. The tone of the essays is sober and restrained. Mascall, in his essay 'Theotokos: The Place of Mary in the Work of Salvation', distinguishes between Jesus Christ and Mary, and also between the terms, 'redemptor' and 'co-redemptor' as well as between 'co-redemptrix' and 'redemptrix'. Mascall writes, 'He is *redemptor*, not *co-redemptor*; she is *co-redemptrix*, not *redemptrix*. The force of the prefix *co* is to indicate not equality but subordination, as when St Paul tells his Corinthian disciples that 'we are God's fellow-workers', his συνεργοι, his *co*-operators. Mary is thus described as co-redemptrix in order to bring out the fact that, while Mary has a real part in the redemptive process, because she is morally and physically associated with her Son, yet her part is, and must be, essentially subordinate and ancillary to his' (p. 19).

This is a careful statement. The distinctions made are delicate and perceptive, especially in terms of 'subordination' and the use of 'ancillary'. But we believe that so careful a statement tends to suggest that it would be theologically unsatisfactory to attempt to identify Mary with the Divine Wisdom. Mascall's sensitive distinctions and the specialized vocabulary he uses in connection with redemption suggest real difficulties in any attempt to bring Mary close to Jesus Christ in His work of Redemption. His special terms have the effect of something like a magnetic disturbance within the field of redemption. We should want to ask questions which probably Mascall did not have in his mind when he wrote and therefore does not feel obliged to answer. We have to ask f the subordinate and ancillary contribution assigned to Mary was essential to Christ's work in Redemption? Would His work have been incomplete or unfinished without her contribution? We think that a negative answer must be returned. Mary is not a redeemer in the sense that Jesus is the Redeemer. In so far then as

Wisdom is correlated with the Redeemer, it becomes improper to identify Wisdom and the Virgin Mary. It is of Jesus Christ only that Divine Wisdom is to be predicated.

The second work is that by Rene Laurentin, an eminent Roman Catholic authority on Mariology, *Mary's Place in the Church* (1964). Laurentin repudiates the extravagant claims made on behalf of Mary, not only in the Roman Catholic Church but also in the Orthodox Church. He rejects them because often they are based on a misuse of Scripture. He singles out for criticism two examples culled from the Orthodox Church, where instead of the New Testament being used on behalf of the divinity of our Lord, the following is written: 'Hail, throne of flame, . . . in you *the fulness of the divinity did dwell corporeally*,' says the Acathistos Hymn, applying to Mary (Col 2:9): '*We have seen her glory, the glory as of the only* Mother of God, *full of grace and truth*,' says Isidoros Glabas, transferring to Mary the words of John 1:14 (p. 132).

Laurentin describes these utterances as 'daring flights of fancy'. What lies behind his criticism here is the truth that all the claims about the Virgin Mary should be controlled by a strict exegesis of the Biblical texts. This principle must be applied, not only to the flights of fancy rightly condemned by Laurentin, but also to that more sophisticated thinking which at present is agitating so many within his own communion. There are very strong differences of opinion in the Roman Catholic Church concerning the relation between the Virgin Mary and the Godhead. Laurentin himself writes, 'In the heat generated by the clash of opposing conceptions, there can be no doubt whatever that there is a tendency, on the one side, to transform Mary into an idol, and, on the other, to turn with horror from this idol'.[1] However,

[1] *Op. cit.*, p. 137.

it seems to us as being quite obvious from the Biblical data that Mary is not to be identified with the Divine Wisdom and that this title is applicable only to Jesus Christ.

The third work is that of Karl Barth, the eminent Protestant theologian, *Church Dogmatics*, Vol. I, part 2, pp. 132–171 (1956). In his discussion of Mariology Barth says, 'every word that makes her person the object of special attention, which ascribes to her what is even a relatively independent part in the drama of salvation, is an attack upon the miracle of revelation' (p. 140). He criticizes the work of M. J. Scheeben, who maintained that it was necessary that someone (in this case, Mary) should 'enter actively in the name of all other men into the carrying out of redemption' (p. 144). The interesting point is that Scheeben tries to justify this bold speculation on the basis of an exegesis of some passages in Wisdom Literature. He writes, and we quote from Barth's account of Scheeben, 'The entire content of the passages on the wisdom of God in Prov 8 (the lesson for the feast of the Immaculate Conception), Ecclus 24 (the lesson for the Feast of Mary's Ascension) and Wisd 7 is applied by him to Mary and interpreted as follows: Wisdom in these passages is portrayed "as a person who has gone out from God, is in close relation to the world, exists and acts in the world outside and along with or even under God".' It is 'in the form of a female person that has proceeded from God, i.e. such a person as in virtue of her proceeding from God and her relationship to God stands by God's side in a manner similar to that of a daughter by her father, and exercises over the world an influence similar to that which a mother exerts in a father's house—i.e., as a principle which has proceeded from God, is similar to Him, and is the seat, vessel and instrument of God, for His consummating, quickening and illuminating impact upon the world.'[1]

Barth dismisses this teaching because it involves Mary in what he calls 'a relative rivalry with Christ'. There is no need to prolong this discussion; enough has been said to indicate that Mary should not be identified with the Divine Wisdom.

The brief references to the works mentioned above and our opening references to the rather dubious attribution of mediatorial functions to Mary, relative to functions previously associated with the figure of Wisdom, provide a starting point for our closing remarks. It is important to remember that as early as the second century the Church rejected all attempts to include a female figure or feminine principle in the work of redemption. Gnosticism sought to intrude Wisdom or Sophia. This was rejected for the good reason that Wisdom was not divine in the sense that Jesus Christ was divine. He is true God and true man, which cannot be said of Wisdom. Salvation is found in the Son to whom Mary gave birth, not in Mary herself, nor in Mary represented by the figure of Wisdom, nor any other possible female figure. Further, the New Testament is simple and clear about the relationship between Jesus Christ and Mary. In the opening chapters of Matthew and Luke, Mary modestly points away from herself to her Son. Mary is not depicted as an equal or co-equal in His work of redemption or revelation. Lastly, and to return to the language of Wisdom and Christology, the New Testament has no other view of Mary than that she is a creature, even if the most honoured of all creatures. Mary is not a goddess. Nor is she divine in the sense that the Father or the Son or the Holy Spirit is divine. The question of her being identified in any way

[1] *Op. cit.* p. 144.

with Wisdom simply does not arise within the New Testament teaching about her. It should also be noted that Jesus was not, as it were, *appointed* to the rank of Wisdom, nor adopted as Wisdom, nor did He in some way earn the title because He deserved it. Rather, the ascription of Wisdom to Jesus Christ is part of a statement about Who He is. It belongs to Him as the Pre-existent One, as the only-begotten Son of God, as the Creator and Redeemer. Wisdom finds its fulfilment and completion in Him. This is the testimony of the New Testament; He alone and not Mary is the power and Wisdom of God.

Also, so far as the most recent and authoritative Roman Catholic writings are concerned, it is noteworthy that there is no mention of Mary as *sedes sapientiae* in the discussion on Mariology in the *Schema Constitutiones De Ecclesia*, published in 1964, nor in the English translation, *The Documents of Vatican II*, published 1966.

SELECT BIBLIOGRAPHY

1. TRANSLATIONS OF ANCIENT TEXTS

R. H. Charles (ed.), *Apocrypha and Pseudepigrapha.* 2 vols. (Clarendon Press, 1913).

S. N. Kramer, *History Begins at Sumer* (Thames and Hudson, 2nd ed., 1961).

W. G. Lambert (ed.), *Babylonian Wisdom Literature* (Clarendon Press, 1960).

M. Noth and D. Winton Thomas (edd.), *Wisdom in Israel and in the Ancient Near East*, Supplement to the Vetus Testamentum, vol. III (Brill, Leiden, 1955).

J. B. Pritchard (ed.), *Ancient Near Eastern Texts* (2nd ed., Princeton, 1953).

2. GENERAL

Karl Barth, *Church Dogmatics*, vol. I, Part 2 (T. and T. Clark, 1956).

M. Black, *An Aramaic Approach to the Gospels and Acts* (Clarendon Press, 1946).

Rudolf Bultmann, *Theology of the New Testament* (S.C.M., 1952).

W. D. Davies, *Paul and Rabbinic Judaism* (S.P.C.K., 1948).

J. J. Van Dijk, *La Sagesse Suméro-Accadienne* (Brill, Leiden, 1953).

C. H. Dodd, *The Interpretation of the Fourth Gospel* (Cambridge, 1953).

J. Drummond, *Philo Judaeus*, 2 vols. (Williams and Norgate, 1888).

A. Grillmeier, *Christ in Christian Tradition* (Mowbray, 1965).

J. Klausner, *From Jesus to Paul* (Allen and Unwin, 1946).

H. Kleinknecht and W. Gutbrod, *Law* (Bible Key Words; A. and C. Black, 1962).

W. L. Knox, *Journal of Theological Studies*, vol. xxxviii, July 1937.

R. Laurentin, *Mary's Place in the Church* (Burns and Oates, 1965).

E. L. Mascall and H. S. Box, *The Blessed Virgin Mary* (Darton, Longman and Todd, 1963).

C. G. Montefiore and H. Loewe, *A Rabbinic Anthology* (Macmillan, 1938).

G. F. Moore, *Judaism*, 3 vols. (Cambridge, 1946).

Gerhard von Rad, *Old Testament Theology*, vol. I (Oliver and Boyd, 1962).

O. S. Rankin, *Israel's Wisdom Literature* (T. and T. Clark, 1936).

A. E. J. Rawlinson, *The New Testament Doctrine of Christ* (Longmans, Green, 1926).

A. E. J. Rawlinson (ed.), *Essays on the Trinity and the Incarnation* (Longmans, Green, 1928).

Helmer Ringgren, *Word and Wisdom* (Lund, 1947).

Helmer Ringgren and Walther Zimmerli, *Sprüche-Prediger* (Göttingen, 1962).

A. Robertson and A. Plummer, *II Corinthians* (International Critical Commentary; T. and T. Clark, 1965).

H. H. Rowley (ed.), *The Old Testament and Modern Study* (Clarendon Press, 1951).

J. C. Rylaarsdam, *Revelation in Jewish Wisdom* (Chicago, 1946).

R. B. Y. Scott, *Vetus Testamentum*, vol. X (Brill, Leiden, 1960).

R. N. Whybray, *Wisdom in Proverbs* (S. C.M., 1965).

J. Wood, *Job and the Human Situation* (Bles, 1966).

G. E. Wright (ed.), *The Bible and the Ancient Near East* (Routledge and Kegan Paul, 1961).

INDEX OF BIBLE REFERENCES